MW01170989

"Writing is an exploration. You start from nothing and learn as you go."
—E. L. Doctorow

Also by Mark Teppo

Silence of Angels
Solitaire
The Potemkin Mosaic
Rudolph! He Is the Reason for the Season
The Court of Lies (collection)
Earth Thirst
Heartland
Lightbreaker

THE FOREWORLD SAGA

The Mongoliad (co-authored with Erik Bear, Greg Bear,
Joseph Brassey, Nicole Galland, Cooper
Moo, & Neal Stephenson)
Katabasis (co-authored with Joseph
Brassey, Cooper Moo, & Angus Trim)

The Lion in Chains (co-authored with Angus Trim)
Cimarronin (co-authored with Ellis Amdur,
Charles C. Mann, & Neal Stephenson)

Sinner
Dreamer
Seer
The Beast of Calatrava

JUMP START YOUR NOVEL

a guide by
MARK TEPPO

TEPPOBOX

Jumpstart Your Novel is a practical how-to guide that presents one author's view on the craft of writing. The views expressed herein are his and his alone. Several chapters of this edition were previously published in *Planning, Plotting, and Progress*.

Copyright © 2018 Mark Teppo

All rights reserved, which means that no portion of this publication may be reproduced or transmitted, in any form or by any means, without the express written permission of the author.

This book was printed in the United States of America. It is a TEPPOBOX publication, which falls under the aegis of Firebird Creative (Clackamas, OR).

Seriously. Let's get it right this time . . .

Cover design based on a concept by Darin Bradley
Cover layout by Firebird Creative
Interior Illustrations by Neal Von Flue

Second TEPPOBOX edition: April 2018.

www.teppobox.com

JUMP START YOUR NOVEL

"Almost all good writing begins with terrible first efforts. You have to start somewhere."
—Anne Lamott

TABLE OF CONTENTS

This page is intentionally NOT blank.

THE SITTING DOWN PART

In some books, you'll find a page that is empty except for one line: "This page is intentionally blank." It's a note to let you know that part of the book hasn't been left out, a marker that says, "We meant to do this." But the blank page—intentional or not—is the terrifying reminder of exactly how every book starts.

A blank page. Followed by another one. And then so on, page after page after page.

Or, more accurately in this digital age, you have a single blank page. You can't even scroll down to the next page in your document because it doesn't exist. Your word processing software only gives you one blank page, and a reminder at the bottom of the screen.

"Words: 0; Characters: 0"

It should be easy, right? You've got a whole page to work with. You can write anything you like. You can write down a short list of things you want to accomplish with this project. Though, if you're like me, these lists turn into lists filled with things like "Butter," "Eggs," and "Fruit." Sometimes I do bullet points of Things I'd Rather Be Doing

Than Sitting Here and Staring At This Blank Page. I try to put down enough items that my word processor gives me a second page. Grudgingly. Like it knows that I'm cheating, especially when I start halfway down that first page with **"TITLE GOES HERE."**

Let's be honest: the first page sucks.

And really, it's not just the first page that can suck. Every page has a high suckage potential. Writing a book can feel like you're starting over with every page. Your creative brain—which will not shut up when you're sitting in the office or trying to sleep or doing any number of things other than sitting in front of the keyboard—turns into a sulky five-year-old when you actually get your butt in the writing chair. Every paragraph is a hard-won negotiation with this recalcitrant toddler. Getting a full page? It's like running a marathon. With lead weights attached to your legs. And a basket of angry chickens strapped to your head.

What? You don't have a cluck of the Angry Chickens of Self-Doubt who constantly peck and nag at you?

Oh, but you do now? Sorry about that. Ignore the chickens. It's just your creative brain inventing another excuse not to write. I know. Another fucking excuse. Just in case you were running out.

But, come on. Excuses are easy. And so is lying to yourself. Which is what we just did there.

Let's try something different. Let's go find that unruly five-year-old part of our brain that keeps insisting on being contrary. Let's trick it. Let's say to it: "This page is intentionally blank."

"No, it isn't," the five-year-old says.

"Yes, it is," you say.

"Is not."

"Is too."

"Is not."

And now the foot stomping starts. "Is not! Is not!"

And here we are, on the third page already. Our content counter now reads: "Words: 506; Characters: 2,800." We're what? One half of a percent done with a novel, which is a half percent more than we were a little while ago. Now it's only a matter of another *mumble mumble* more words to go. Easy, right?

Okay, so maybe we're getting ahead of ourselves.

Writing a book takes time. There's no getting around the physical actions required to put words on the page. Even if you've got a certificate from Willie Bob's Online Typing School that says you're the fastest two-finger key-banger who has ever run the gauntlet of their online course, it's still going to take you at least two full days—non-stop, no pee breaks!—to transcribe a novel's worth of words. And this begs the question of whether that book is ready to come out of your brain as fast as your fingers can go. Writing takes time, and the biggest complaint every writer has when they are starting out is *Who has the time?*

Which is the wrong thing to complain about. There's always enough time. What you're struggling with is the lack of a plan. You need a way to use your time effectively—no matter how fragmented and scattered these hours and minutes are.

And that bring us to this book. The title says we're going to do some serious jumpstarting, and so we should get to that, shouldn't we?

Are you ready?

"No, I'm not."

Ah, that fucking five-year old in your head. Always keeping you from making the most of yourself. Well, tape that kid to the wall. If you've got any of those chickens of self-doubt running around, drive them out of the room and close the door. Just let go of all those excuses.

Let's do this.

I know you've got the good stuff in there. Let it out!

THE WRITING PART

THIS BOOK WILL NOT WRITE YOUR NOVEL FOR YOU.

God, I'm a bastard. I got you all excited on the previous page, and then I sucker-punch you. It's so very mean of me, but it had to be done. You must lose yourself, grasshopper, before you can become yourself—or some such nonsense.

Here's the thing: regardless of all those emails from sparkly-eyed, shark-toothed hucksters who claim have the secret to "HOW BOOKS WRITE THEMSELVES," the truth of the matter is a book gets written because someone shows up and does the work. And we've done that, right? We're in our favorite chair. All ready to go and . . .

And, there's a bit more to it than that, and we're going to ease into it. We are going to start with a blank page, zap a bit of electrical current into our brains (metaphorically speaking, of course), and make an outline. And then we'll refine it a bit. And then a bit more. Eventually, you'll reach a point where you'll wave me off. "I got this," you'll say. "Now leave me the fuck alone and let me do this."

That is your brain on fire. That's our true goal.

Now, a caveat. Of course. The model outlined in this book (what I like to call the "Nine Box Outline Model" when I am feeling particularly proud of myself) is a process model, which is to say that it works for most people, but not all. You may be weird and not like all the other kids, which is fine. I still like you, but you're going to make *that* face a lot as we work through this. I know, I know. But stick with it. After we do the NBOM, we'll address a few other things, which might help snap everything into focus.[1]

But first, let's talk a moment about two core styles of outlining and preparation. These are . . .

PANTSING VS PLODDING

Generally, there are two camps when it comes to talking about how to write a book: making things up as you go (the pantser model)[2], or following a very strict outline (the plodder—er, the plotter—model). Neither is better than the other. Really. I know this is going to disappoint some of you who were hoping this was one of the secrets. Pantsing isn't it, sorry. Plodder isn't the magic bean, either.

Here is a not-entirely daft observation, though: You may switch from being one to the other over the course of your

---

1. If not, well, you can always use the pages from this book to make paper airplanes, or feed it to your dog, or several hundred other things you can do with a writing book that failed to give you all the answers. Though, I bet "sit the fuck down and write" is still good advice, regardless of how the rest turns out. Just saying.
2. Wearing actual pants while writing (or not) does not make you a pantser (or not). Different thing entirely. Truly.

writing career. It's not quite the same as switching from one diametrically opposed political party to another or making the switch from beer to wine or to harder spirits. It's more like admitting to yourself after years of drinking coffee that you really don't like the acrid taste, and you're going to switch to tea. Hallelujah! Confetti from the sky! Rainbows smacking you in the eyeballs!

Sure, you have to break the news to your three friends who all chipped in to buy Clover machine that you're sharing between households, and they'll probably stop talking to you for several months until they realize that they only have to share the machine with two other people instead of three, but honestly? Your stomach lining is no longer revolting, and that nasty twitch in your left hand that had been causing a number of double 'e' and 's' characters in your manuscripts has gone away.

And six months from now, one of the other three will accidentally have tea when he's at your place, and he'll confess that he liked it and could you recommend some varieties he might want to stock at his house for when you visit? And you'll be kind and write the names down—without a twitch of self-righteous validation—and then you'll give him a hug because you know the tea isn't really for you, but change is hard, and none of us should have to do it alone. Even though you did, and those ungrateful assholes totally shut you out during the first months when you woke up in the middle of the night—the sheets soaked with sweat, your mouth dry and head pounding, and your hands fixed in claw shapes. Shaking from coffee withdrawals.

Like I said, it'll happen once—maybe twice—during your writing career. It's okay if it does. It probably means you're growing as a writer or some other nonsense.[3]

Do pansters really make it all up as they go? No. Well, yes. But no. They don't plan ahead. At least, not very far ahead. They like to allow a book to grow organically. They don't worry overmuch about structure and what the ending is going to be or whether the boy gets the girl or the girl gets the other girl or the boy gets the alien mutt. They just put the characters in an interesting situation, stir, and write down what happens next. Sometimes it works. Sometimes it is a real mess.

I happen to like writing. I don't consider outlining to be writing. I consider it the dull boring slog of playing *What if?* all day and making notes. And I know that as soon as I actually put the characters in this *What if?* situation that I've come up with, they're going to have a different reaction than I planned, and all my notes aren't going to do diddly. So I spin them up and get out of the way.

Does that mean that I occasionally spin up a situation that doesn't work out and have to backtrack and start over? Yes, it does. Does that suck? Yes, it does. Am I the only one who does it this way? No, I am not. I'm not going to name names, but a writer of ginormously successful fantasy novels is a bit of a panster from what I can discern from his conversations about his process. None of his fans

---

3. Hell, between the first edition of this book and the second, I started to rethink my slavish devotion to being a panster. I'm not putting them or taking them off, so to speak, I'm merely considering my options.

are terribly happy about this. I can assure you that he isn't either. But it is his process.

I feel his pain. I do.

I can get away with pantsing because I write fast. I'm working on a novel at the same time I'm writing this nonfiction book. I've hit a wall for the second time and need to back up. All the way to the beginning. I'm dumping 60,000 words. Again. Is this a big deal? Sort of. I've only been working on this book for six months. Does this mean my planning is bad and that I didn't think through all nine boxes before I started? Probably. Will I still finish the book in nine months after I started? Probably. Was I efficient? Hmmm. Not terribly so.[4]

Here's the first truism I'm going to hit you with: the definition of a good book is a book that is finished. That's the only quality assessment you can assign to a WIP[5]: Is it done? *Yes* or *No*? If the answer is *no*, then sit the fuck back down and write some more.

Plodders—er, *Plotters*—want to know what they're doing before they start. A wildly successful science fiction writer I know spends a better part of a year thinking about his book. Just thinking. Lots of "big brain action with no words coming out" sort of thinking. And then, when he's got the book all squared away in his head, he starts to

---

4. This was *Thrush*, if I recall correctly, and I dumped another 30,000 or so before I finally finished a draft. And it took me—all together—about fourteen months to finish that draft. Granted, I put it aside for awhile in there, but still . . . not my best effort on the efficiency front.

5. *Work in Progress*. Writer shorthand. Not dissimilar to WAFU—*Work All Fucked Up*, which happens more often than any of us like, right?

write. And he writes at, like, a hundred thousand words an hour. Four months later, he's finished his latest door-stopper of an SF novel. Total time spent? Probably a year. Number of times he had to start over? Zero.

It's hard to say which is better. Plotters are probably more efficient, but boy, I like writing. Thinking about writing sounds like a dull way to spend an afternoon.

The intent of this book is not just to swear a lot about writing, but to also help you put together a bare-bones outline that will not only give us eager pantsers something to work from when we do actually sit down and write, but it will be enough to make even the ploddiest of plotters marginally happy. See? We're attempting to bridge the gap. Isn't it sweet?

I'm not diminishing or downplaying the effectiveness of the plotter model. The Nine Box Outline Model gives you a whole bunch of material in just a few hours. What you do with it next is entirely up to what sort of writer you are. But you have material to work with, and that is the critical part of getting started. You need to have enough material that you'll feel confident to take the next step, whether it is the start of a quick sprint or the steady methodical pace of Those Who Finish, Eventually.

And it is only Those Who Finish (Eventually or Other-wise) who gets to say: "Why, yes, I have written a *good* book because I finished the fucking thing."

We all want to be Those Who Finish, don't we?

So let's get to it.

PART ONE

THE
OUTLINING

THE NINE BOX MODEL

THE NINE BOX OUTLINE MODEL IS PRETTY SIMPLE. YOU take a piece of paper and draw nine boxes on it. It'll look something like what's on the verso page over there.

The Nine Box Model is a method of organizing your thoughts in a way that separates them from each other. While not all thoughts are distinct units, many of them benefit from a little breathing room.

We all make To Do lists. Back when I was chained to a cubicle, the hip thing in corporate world was daily planners with regimented systems of listing things that you needed to do each day. Every morning you were supposed to take ten minutes and reflect on what you wanted to accomplish that day, and write all these things down. And then you were supposed to look back at the day before and transfer all the things you didn't accomplish to today's list. Within a week, I gave up on this method. My lists from day-to-day were always longer than I could accomplish, and by the end of the week, I needed two or three pages to track everything I hadn't gotten done yet. It was horribly depressing.

The same thing is true with the state of any number of storage spaces scattered around the house. A list of the projects in those spaces would be very long, and I'd look at it, sigh, and then recycle the piece of paper.

Long lists are tiring. They wear you out by their mere presence. They are always longer than the amount of time you will ever have, and your natural inclination is to give up before you start.

Writing a novel is not dissimilar, especially when you are starting with a blank page. It'll take months. There's so much research to do. You don't know who the characters are. You need to clean the garage. Feed your kids/spouse/self. Vacuum the cat. Put on clothes and leave the house once a week so that your neighbors don't think you've died. So much to do. It can be very difficult to get started.

Here's the trick. You can only put one foot in front of the other. You can only write one word at a time. Everything is a sequence that, over time, accumulates effort and work. The book gets done because you put in the time. It's nice to lounge about and think, "Oh, wow. Won't it be nice when this book is done, and my publisher starts backing up the armored cars full of cash?"

But part of your brain will whine, and say, "Yes, but when is that going to happen?"

"Well, as soon as I finish the book," you'll answer back.

"And when is that going to happen?" your brain will fire back as it dumps the entire list of Things That Must Be Done In Order For The Book To Be Finished into your lap.

And that's when the panic sets in.

Let's ignore the panic. Let's focus on one thing at a time. That's what the Nine Box Model is all about. There is lots of research data that says we—as a species—really can't multitask all that well, and the torrential rise of social media distractions aren't helping. You can't write a book, vacuum the cat, and cook a gourmet meal simultaneously. Not well, at any rate.

My dear pal Neal Von Flue has been kind enough to draw up some clever pictures for the boxes, so let's take a moment and regale ourselves with them.

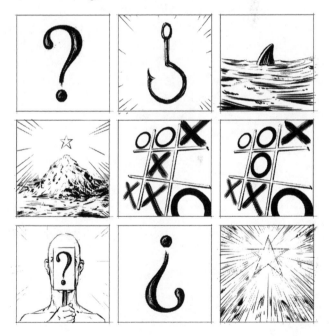

Right. So each box represents a single aspect of the novel. We're going to step through each of these boxes, and spend a little time talking about what that box represents and how you can frame some brainstorming around the contents of that box.

Don't worry too much about what the icons mean right now. We'll get to them. For the moment, this is a game plan. Nine boxes. Nine steps. One book. The separation afforded us by the boxes means that we have permission to focus on doing one thing at a time, which means we can do that one thing with all of our attention.

Everything else—the horribly unvacuumed cat, the dishes in the sink, the neglected spouse wandering around the house making that weird noise—none of those things are important right now. Why not? Because they're not part of what you are doing RIGHT NOW. They'll be there later. Oh, yes, they will. But for now, all we've got are these nine boxes to fill.

Let's get started . . .

THE PROTAGONIST

ATLAS SHRUGGED BEGINS WITH A QUESTION: "WHO IS John Galt?" Well, we don't know because we just opened this book, so asking US the question is kind of like being invited to a party, and when you show up, the host opens the door and asks: "What's in the refrigerator?" There could be a half-wheel of moldy cheese, a six-pack of microbrew beer, some floppy carrots, or even a severed head. Who the fuck knows, right?

It's kind of a cheap question to throw at a reader from the get-go like that, but the flipside of that initial ask is that you are now wondering who John Galt is, aren't you? Even though you're a bit annoyed, you're going to read the next sentence at least. Just like the obnoxious host at the door, now that the question has been asked, you want to know: what's in the refrigerator.[6]

---

6. In the case of *Atlas Shrugged*, though, the light in the refrigerator has gone out and you have to root around to find anything; even then, you're not sure if what you've found is a cabbage or a moss-covered head.

Even though you are the author of this book, at this stage in the creative process (which is to say: five seconds after getting a blank piece of paper and sharpening your pencil), this is the question you need to ask yourself: Who is your protagonist?

Protagonists come in so many different varieties that we'd be here all month trying to list them all, and it's not necessary to do so, really. I like Merriam-Webster's second definition for protagonist: "an important person who is involved in a competition, conflict, or cause." The first one—"the main character in a novel, play, movie, etc."—is fine, but there's an important distinction here that I want to highlight.

Let's look at that definition again, and tweak it slightly.

> *Your protagonist is an important character, whose involvement in a conflict is critical to your story.*

The other definition merely states that the protagonist is a "main" character. Well, what defines "main"?

Lots of lines?

Lots of page time?

A big dramatic death scene?

Let's go to that old hoary standard, J. R. R. Tolkien's *The Lord of the Rings*.

There are a dozen "main" characters, scattered throughout the book. Are they all the protagonist? Sure, if you want to split hairs, but one of them is more critical than the others. That's your true protagonist.

It's Frodo.

Not Sam. Or Gandalf. Or Boromir. It's Frodo Baggins. The every-hobbit.

And yes, there are many other characters who have interesting stories in *The Lord of the Rings*. And many other books have many other narrative strands, and that's all very clever, but let's keep it simple for now. We're going to keep the focus on one protagonist as we move through this outline process. Because too much cleverness early on makes for an outline that resembles a sketch of an octopus trying to flee the scene of a crime.[7]

Now, how much do you need to know about that individual before you start writing the book? That all depends on whether you are a pantser or a plotter.

A panster will probably write: "Tall, sexy, blue eyes, doesn't like noisy dogs or overripe tomatoes. Knows how to throat punch a rabid poodle." And that's good enough.

A plotter will probably want to spend sixteen weeks, detailing an intricate amount of information about this character's backstory: who was their first love; what kind of eduction did they have, and how good were they at it; what was their first pet's name; where did they grow up; why is Daddy crying out in the garage all the time; what their first job was; how many jelly beans did they steal

---

7. Also, each of these other characters are the protagonists of their own story, even if it is only so in their own minds. You know what this means, don't you? Running through this exercise for each of these characters in your story. I know, headache inducing. Let's leave that alone for now.

from the treat plate at the orphanage during the holiday pageant last year. All those sorts of things and probably sixteen dozen more. It's okay if you don't care about all those details. Most of your readers won't either, but some writers like to know these things before they put on the skin of this character and make it dance around on the page.[8]

The right answer—and not that there is a right answer, but if there was one, this would be it—is that you should know as much about your protagonist as you feel is necessary for you to be able to transcribe their actions, reactions, motivation, fears, and desires that come about in any given situation where they are subject to external stimuli.

Say what?

How much do you need to know before you can convincingly fake being that character?

There's your answer.

And here's the important thing to remember: most of what you write down about this character at this stage may never show up on the page. That's okay. Know enough to fake it, and know that confidence comes from faking.

Mostly. And I'm not lying there.

---

8. I'm going to refer to singular individuals like the Protagonist with a plural pronoun for two reasons: 1) I don't want to assign a gender to your Protagonist, but writing "the Protagonist" over and over again is going to be tedious to read; and 2) the use of alternating "he" and "she" pronouns makes my brain think that we're talking about different people when we're not. The *Chicago Manual of Style* says I have wiggle room in this regard, so we're going to wiggle.

EXERCISE

We have reached that point in the process where it is time for me to stop yammering and for you to do some writing. The Protagonist is the first box in our Nine Box Outline Model. Give yourself five to ten minutes. Write down everything that comes to mind when you ask yourself this question: *Who is your protagonist?*

Be as detailed as you like. Be as general as you are lazy. Just write for the entire time you've given yourself. Describe the character. Describe the character's house. Their preferred mode of transportation. Who are their friends? Are they alive or dead? Why? Does your character have any pets? Why not? What happened to your protagonist's mother and father? Did they have parents? What's their favorite color? What's their favorite TV show? Would they eat a Twinkie if they were coming off an eighty-day hunger strike and all they were given was a plate full of the deliciously moist and not made from real ingredients snack cakes? Ask yourself as many questions as you need, and let them get silly, because sometimes you really find out something interesting about someone when you ask them a silly question.

And if you're not the type to subject someone you barely know to a special interrogation session, then draw a picture of your character instead. Or draw a picture of a unicorn because that's what your protagonist would do when asked to describe themselves. Write a song your protagonist likes to sing. A song they like to hate.

Spend five to ten minutes getting to know this person because you're going to be spending a lot of time with them. Give them foibles. Give them secret powers. Give them hopes and fears. Aspirations. Love. Frustration. Anger. Give them the secret word that unlocks the heart of the universe and watch what they do with it. Invite them into your house and secretly watch what they do when they think you're in the kitchen, fixing up a cocktail. What sort of cocktail would they ask for?

Don't stop to think about anything else for the duration of the timer. Just write stuff down about your protagonist. We'll filter later. Right now? We're just making stuff up.

This is the best part of what we do, after all.

And when you are done, let's move on to . . .

THE HOOK

CONSIDER THESE TWO OPENINGS.

ONE:

> *"Let's go fishing this week," my dad announced at Sunday dinner.*
>
> *"Okay!" I was excited to spend some time with my father. Since I had gotten back from college a few weeks ago, we had both been busy with our lives. He'd been working on a special project that involved putting cats in a centrifuge to see how fast they could spin and still land on their feet, and I'd been trying to catch up with Doug and Ralph and Tito—my old pals from high school.*
>
> *"How about Tuesday?" my dad said.*
>
> *"Tuesday is great," I replied. "I just need to find my fishing rod."*

"It should be out in the garage," my dad said. "But you'll probably have to re-reel the line."

"Okay," I said. Well, I knew what I was going to be doing Monday morning. Hauling a hundred yards of fishing line out of a reel and stretching it out across the lawn to make sure that it was still good. If it was tangled at all, I'd be there awhile, picking at tiny knots with my fingers.

"Oh, and we'll need to go pick nightcrawlers," my dad said. "I think the funeral home down on Ascot waters their lawn on Monday. We'll go tomorrow night, after sundown. Get some worms."

"Okay," I said, my enthusiasm waning a bit. Monday night? Geez, there went the whole day. I had been hoping to hang out with Ralph and smoke some weed. Maybe try to play that new first-person shooter while baked. And maybe Alison, his sister, might be around. Boy, she was something else . . .

Two:

On Tuesday afternoon, under a sky filled with clouds like steel wool, I hooked a monster.

Cat centrifuging aside, which opening throws you into the story more? It's entirely possible that Opening Two happens four or five pages past Opening One, but are you going to make it that far?

William Goldman, in his book *Which Lie Did I Tell?*, says that we must strive to "enter all scenes as late as possible."[9]

Kurt Vonnegut, in his prefatory remarks to his 1999 collection, *Bagombo Snuff Box*, lists eight rules for writing. The fifth rule is: "Start as late as possible."[10]

Keep these rules in mind as you work through your outline. They're not just critical to the Hook; they're important in nearly every scene. What event happens at the beginning of your novel that hooks your reader?

I gave Ayn Rand a hard time about her opening line to *Atlas Shrugged* in the last chapter, but let's look at it again in light of the Hook.

"Who is John Galt?"

Well, we know that Ayn Rand knows who John Galt is, right? She's not free associating and literally making up the book as she types out the words. She knows all about John Galt, and while the question is rhetorical for her, it's a hook for the reader. Who is this guy? Why is he important? As a reader, why should I care? Those questions all hit you like a speeding truck, and you're only four words into the book. Are you going to keep reading?

Damn straight you are.

Let's look at *Die Hard*, the movie that forever changed the testosterone action film landscape and transformed Bruce Willis's career overnight. It begins with New York Detective John McClane showing some nerves while his

9. *Which Lie Did I Tell?: More Adventures in the Screen Trade* (Vintage, 2001), p. 198.
10. On page 10 of the G. P. Putnam's Sons edition, in fact.

plane lands in LA. In the first two minutes of screen time, we learn that he's a control freak, who doesn't like heights, and he's a smart-ass. Shortly thereafter, he meets Argyle, the young and earnest driver of the limo that has been sent to pick him up. Once they're underway, Argyle grills him about why he's in LA, whereupon we learn that he's separated from his wife and this trip is an effort to patch up a marriage that has been on the rocks for some time. Mostly because of his ego, we suspect.

In between, though, we get a scene with his wife, Holly, where we learn that she's apprehensive about his visit as well, but hopes that they can work things out.

All of this is accomplished without either character talking to one another. But we know all about their conflict, and we're hooked into what is going to happen when they do finally see each other.[11]

Recently, I ran through this model with a number of eighth grade students. Not surprisingly, they had all read Suzanne Collins's *Hunger Games*.

"How does that book start?" I asked the class.

Finally, a wee voice spoke up: "Katniss was out hunting."

"That's not all *that* interesting," I said. "Something else?"

Another voice piped up: "She wasn't supposed to be hunting."

"That's a little better," I said. "But . . ."

From the front row: "She had a boy with her."

"And is that enough to keep your interest?" I asked.

---

11. Check out Appendix B in the back for a full breakdown of *Die Hard* in light of the Nine Box Outline Model.

Finally, from the back: "Her sister Prim gets chosen at the Reaping."

Bingo!

The Reaping. And not just any dull, everyday sort of reaping. A capital-R sort of *Reaping*. The sort of event that happens once or twice in a lifetime sort of *Reaping*.[12] Where Katnis volunteered to take Prim's place.

Do you see what just happened there?

Hook + Protagonist = Narrative Drive.

We want to know what happens next. And how much do we really know about the world where Katniss and Prim live? How much do we know about Katniss? How much does it matter?

Katniss's sister is in danger, and Katniss steps in to save her. That's what matters. That's the Hook.

You'll be told you need to hook your readers on the first line. I think that's extreme. You'll be told that you have to give them a reason to turn the page, or they'll wander off. That's true, to a point.

If, while you're standing in line at the grocery store, you pick up and page through paperbacks stuffed in the racks around you, you'll probably find that none of them hook you fast with either the first line or the first page. Authors who have published a few books get a bit of leeway in this regard (Stephen King with *Bag of Bones*, for example: he doesn't really set the hook until the last page of the first

---

12. Or every year, in the case of *The Hunger Games*, because, you know, compression of attention spans and all. It gets harder and harder to get folks engaged.

chapter, but wow, does he set the hook deep!), and you will too, once you've had a few books published.

The real critical function of the first page is that it demonstrates that you can write a compelling opening. Forcing a hook in the first line or page can result in tortured setups that end up obscuring the narrative more than actually hooking the reader. If you kick up mud along the bottom of the river, the fish can't see the bait. Keep your writing tight and clear. Lead us to the hook. We'll give you a little bit of time, but only if you demonstrate that you know what you're doing.

In both *Die Hard* and *The Hunger Games*, we got a bit of world-building and narrative grounding before we got the hook. We got the *Who?* before we got the *What?* A hand that reaches out of the shadows and smacks you is shocking, but it leaves you disoriented. Seeing someone put on the glove before they disappear into the darkness leaves you thinking: *Hey, now, what's going on here?*

Here's one more example. George Miller recently returned to his Mad Max world with *Fury Road*, a movie that has, much like *Die Hard* did many years ago, upset the cinematic landscape. The film opens with a long iconic shot of a hooded figure standing next to a souped-up muscle car. The landscape is sere and orange. Desert wasteland. We get a touch of voice-over monologue. Which is doing what? That's right, introducing our protagonist.[13]

---

13. Okay, okay. I know that Max isn't truly the film's protagonist, but what Miller is doing here is grounding the audience. The film is called *Mad Max*, for crying out loud. There is an understanding that a good portion

Thirty seconds later, bad guys show up. A big chase scene occurs, which runs us through an entire inventory of visual cues and cinematic language that we're going to have to rely heavily on for the next two hours because there's just not a whole lot of dialogue in this film. Max tries to escape, almost makes it, and is pulled back into the hellhole that he was trying to break free of.

Boom. Title card. Big noisy chrome title card.

Go take a look at one of the trailers for the film. They basically replicate the opening minutes of the film, which I've described here. Given what you see in the trailer, how much do you know about the plot of the film? Who are the characters? What sort of world do they live in? What are the stakes?

These are the questions your readers are going to ask, but right now? They don't care, because they are hooked. [14]

---

of the audience will remember the first three films. He's setting us up for the first act reversal. He knows what he is doing, and he gets a pass, so let's not get distracted by what's really happening here. Let's pretend that it is exactly the sort of narrative that he wants us to think it is.

14. Max is trying to escape from being branded in the opening chase sequence. What's the first thing we see after his failed attempt and the noisy title card? We see the brand on the back of someone's neck. When the camera pulls back, we see that we've been looking at the back of Furiosa's neck. We're now getting to meet the true protagonist of the story, which isn't Max. What Miller has done by showing us her brand is that he's just told us that she has already suffered through everything that we saw Max trying to flee. And so when she cranks the wheel of the War Machine and heads off course, we don't have to be told why she's doing it because, down in our guts, we know why.

EXERCISE

This time, let's write down what's going on when the novel starts. What's the Protagonist doing that is going to hook us into their story?

Remember that we're still operating in our discrete boxes, and the only one we've filled out so far is the Protagonist box. Whatever is happening in the book is interesting and fascinating because of how the Protagonist is dealing with this situation. We may not know the reasons why things are happening. We may not know very much about the world yet. But the Hook shows us something about the Protagonist that makes us want to read more.

The Hook is the macro view in comparison to the micro view of the Protagonist. Imagine that you've started with a tight close-up focus on the Protagonist. Just long enough for the readers to get a good sense of who they are. Then, you pull back to show us what's going on around the Protagonist.

Here's an example: Tim is sitting in a chair, at a wooden desk that looks like one of those old school desks. Tim needs a haircut, and he's wearing a T-shirt with some clever hipster saying on it. There's a pad of paper on the desk in front of him. He's got a pen. He's clicking the end of it. *Click. Click. Clickity-click-click.*

We pull back and find that Tim is sitting in a sparse room somewhere, surrounded by other desks, which are filled with people just as nervous as he is. Some are younger. Some are older. Some are more worried than he is. There's a guy two seats over from Tim who looks bored half to death. He probably doesn't even have a pen.

There's a clock on the wall. The second hand is ten minutes shy of the top of the hour. Judging from everyone's level of perspiration and panic, they've got about ten minutes left before something happens.

What is going to happen?

We're going to need a little more to answer that question, aren't we? Let's add something to the mix. Let's move on the next box, where we meet . . .

THE ADVERSARY

ANY STORY IS FUNDAMENTALLY A STORY ABOUT CONFLICT. Two people (at minimum) want different things, and as they attempt to reach these goals, they run afoul of each other. Usually one is designated the hero and the other is designated the villain. Many villains dislike being categorized as such (because, in their heads, they are the protagonist of their own story), and will push back against such lazy labeling.

I've been careful to not label the protagonist the "hero," because we have this delightful cynical trend in modern literature of the "anti-hero." This individual may exhibit qualities which disqualify them for sainthood, but in most cases, they are merely a lesser of evils confronting the world. In some extreme cases, the anti-hero is really just an asshole who gets a book written about them.

There's always an outlier.

Regardless, we're going to use more generic terms when we outline because we don't want to get caught thinking that any given character must perform in a certain role within the book. It makes us predisposed to do certain things that are lazy, frankly. And we, most certainly, are not the lazy type.

So, with this in mind, we shall define the Adversary as merely That Which Is In Conflict With The Protagonist. It may be a person. It may be a wild natural force. It may be an entity with many agents. It may be unformed chaos, sneaking in through a hole in time/space. Again, by not using "villain" or "antagonist," we're merely trying to avoid putting any *a priori* models into this box.

In *The Hunger Games*, Katniss volunteers to take her sister's place in the Reaping. She'll participate in the Games that are sponsored by the Capitol. The Capitol is given a face in President Snow and in various other characters who interact with Katniss throughout the novel (and its two sequels). We could narrow our definition of the Adversary to any of these characters, but each of them are adversarial only in specific portions of the novel. The Adversary we want to identify here is the ultimate agency who wants something counter to the Protagonist's goal.[15]

Now, we're just about to finish up the first row of boxes of the model. We will have the top tier of three—one third of the structure of the novel. We should be feeling confident enough in our wild brainstorming powers to start

---

15. In this instance, I'll argue that the Adversary is the entire culture that has created a world were the Hunger Games is acceptable. The Capitol and President Snow are personified aspects of the Adversary's nature. To get all academic on you.

thinking about these individual boxes in relation to each other. With the Hook, we considered it as the macro to the Protagonist's micro view, and we'll continue pulling back with the Adversary box.

This is the *huzzabuzzawha?* view.

That's a very technical term. The *huzzabuzzawha?*

Let's go back to our previous example with Tim, sitting at a wooden desk. He's nervous. We pull back and see that he's in a classroom environment with other students who are equally nervous. They're all watching the clock. We pull back even farther now, and we see that this classroom is on a floating island in the middle of an ocean, which is filled with ravenous sharks.

Huzzabuzzawha?

This example is nonsensical mainly to make a point, which is that even when you introduce the Adversary, you still aren't revealing all of the world you're building. You're only revealing the shape of the conflict that is to come because while the Hook is related to the novel that you're writing, the Hook is not the only obstacle the Protagonist is going to overcome. The Hook works on its own, without us knowing anything more about the world or the forces that will ultimately come to bear against the Protagonist.

The Hook hooks us; the Adversary sustains us once the sharp shock of the Hook wears off.

In *Die Hard,* the Hook is John and Holly's relationship, which gets summarily set on hold when the Adversary shows up and blows Mr. Takagi's head off.

Huzzabuzzawha?

We need to know who the Adversary is at this point in our planning. We need to know who is going to get in the Protagonist's way for the next couple of hundred pages. The reader probably won't know the Adversary as well as we do, but they'll know the Adversary is out there.

This is the mystery we tease to our readers. They know there's more world to be revealed. It might not all make sense at first glance, but by this point in the book, they're willing to trust the author a little bit.

It's the *huzzabuzzawha?* feeling of not knowing how all these pieces work together, but wanting to keep turning pages until you find out how and why and what-for.

EXERCISE

Give yourself five to ten minutes to brainstorm and write on the Adversary. It will be difficult to not conceive of the Adversary as a mirror or foil to the Protagonist, and that's fine. But spend a few minutes thinking about the Adversary's desires. They don't exist merely to conflict with the Protagonist.

A huge part of the narrative tension in your book is the fact that the Adversary and the Protagonist are at odds with one another, but very rarely is this opposition known to either party prior to the book beginning.

Unless your Adversary is Professor Moriarity, and he's laying a trap for Sherlock Holmes.

But for most of us, the Adversary is merely trying to achieve their own goal (protaging their own novel, right?), and this pesky "villain" keeps getting in their way. It's important that the Adversay has their own plan (which is their goal) and their own agency (how they're going to achieve that goal). Once you realize these details, then it will become easier to examine the ways in which the Protagonist and the Adversary will interact.

Once you've given yourself some time to become familiar with the Adversary, let's move on to the second row of the Nine Box model and consider what the Protagonist wants . . .

THE GOAL

THE GOAL BOX IS THE FIRST BOX OF THE SECOND TIER of the Nine Box Outline Model. As we worked across the first row, not only did we consider each box by itself, but we also considered them as a series of three that gave us a richer understanding of the world we were building, though mostly from the point of view of two characters. There is a linear left-to-right progression that went on: from the micro to the macro to the *huzzabuzzawha?* This progression also holds true as we descend down the first column of boxes.

The first column is the column of boxes where we step back from the work and consider aspects of the book that may not show up on the page. But they are important aspects of the story that we—as the author—need to have a solid understanding of. As I mentioned at the end of the discussion regarding the Adversary box, we're getting to that point in the story where we need to know what the protagonist wants.

The reason we're asking this question here instead of at the beginning is because we have been breaking down the constituent parts of this book into quantifiable chunks. A novel is a sprawling monstrosity that has many, many moving parts. When you're staring at a blank page and you don't know where (or how) to start, you have to tackle the work in smaller pieces.

When we defined the Protagonist, was it necessary to know what they wanted? No. Could we have given them their goal in the first box? Sure. In *Die Hard*, John McClane states his goal in the first few minutes of the film. All he wants is to be reconciled with his wife. But then Hans Gruber shows up and everything changes, right? McClane gets Hooked and meets his Adversary. What's his Goal now?

The smart-ass answer is "Survive," and in many cases, that will be the basic goal state of any protagonist. But you need to strip away the facile answer and dig a little deeper. In McClane's case, his goal is not only to rescue his wife (Duh!) but also to do his job. Why? Because what John McClane really wants is for his wife to know that he wasn't an asshole who ignored her, but that he's just an average guy trying to do a decent job of being a hero for those who can't defend themselves. The world just keeps throwing more and more ludicrous hurdles in his way (read the rest of the *Die Hard* films).[16]

---

16. As an aside, notice which of the films are the most coherent in their explanation of McClane's true goal and how that goal creates a sustainable narrative tension. It's the films where his goal is personal and relatable. We

What is Katniss's goal in *The Hunger Games*? It's not just to survive the Games; it's to bring down the Capitol. She may not realize this immediately—and, in fact, it's not even on the readers' radar in the first book—but the author knew this was Katniss's ultimate goal. Katniss had other short-term goals to achieve, and those goals are what make up the second act of the story (and what help set the stage for the sequels).

Shortly after we articulate who the Adversary is, we need to know what the protagonist's ultimate goal is.

In William Shakespeare's play, *Hamlet*, the titular prince is lured out onto the battlements of the castle at Elsinore where the ghost of his father commands Hamlet to "revenge his foul and most unnatural murder" (line 761). By line 840, Hamlet is on board with this program, and a little over 3,200 lines later, the deed is done. Hamlet tends to be loquacious, so the percentage may seem a little off, but at about the 20% mark, we've got a Protagonist (mawkish Danish prince) who has been Hooked (the ghost of his dad shows up, moaning about being murdered), and we know the Adversary (Hamlet's uncle and mom) as well as Hamlet's goal.[17]

The rest, as they say backstage, is giving the audience what they paid for.

---

know what he wants, and that doesn't change throughout the course of the film. (This would be I, II, and IV; notice the difference in how the immediacy of this goal affects the course of the story.)

17. "And thy commandment all alone shall live / Within the book and volume of my brain, / Unmix'd with baser matter."

EXERCISE

You've probably been writing for anywhere from fifteen minutes to a half hour already, and filling out this box can be a little less rigorous. Give yourself half as much time as you have been using (three to five minutes), and in broad strokes, write out the protagonist's goal for the period of time covered by this story. It's not the goal for how they address the Hook because the solution of that problem is what gets the reader past the Hook and into the story.

We have to reach a little deeper now. What does the Protagonist want after they've met the Adversary? You don't need to spell it out on the page early in the book, but the author needs to know the answer to this question soon, as it will impact how the protagonist approaches the series of adventures known as . . .

OBSTACLES & OPPORTUNITIES

THE OTHER TWO BOXES ON THE SECOND TIER ARE distinct from one another, but we're going to talk about them as a related pair. They are the Obstacles and the Opportunities that are presented to the protagonist. There will be more than one set. Traditional wisdom says there are three. This can be a trap. However, the part of the human brain that clings to the familiar likes it when things happen in threes. I'm sure there's a study somewhere which says why in great neurological and sociological detail, but let's not overthinking and stick with the rule of three.

We're breaking the rules here, I know. I told you that we'd be working these boxes one by one, and that we'd be staying within each box as we went. Yet, here we are, cresting the halfway point, and I'm telling you a) these next two boxes are tied together, and b), they'll happen more than once. Why am I doing this?

Because of something called the Three Act Structure.[18]

It's a Hollywood term, and it states that every film has a three part structure: a setup, conflict & further conflict, and a resolution that is tied off by a conclusion. The three acts are not equal in length; they are, in fact, 25% / 50% / 25%.

Look at our three tier structure of the Nine Box outline model. The top tier—where we identified Protagonist, Hook, and Adversary—is the first quarter of your narrative. The bottom tier (which we'll get to soon enough) is the last 25% of your story. The middle tier—which is Goal, Obstacles, and Opportunities—is the largest portion of your story. It's half.

Why?

Because your protagonist must try and fail several times in their quest to achieve their goal.

Let's go back to our steadfast example of *Die Hard*. At thirty-one minutes into the film, Hans Gruber kills one of the Nakatomi executives, shocking everyone and letting them know he means very deadly business. John McClane, who had been luxuriating in the feeling of shag carpet underneath his bare feet, witnesses the execution and must flee for his life.[19]

Where does Hamlet learn of his father's most untimely death? Does it change his world completely and start

---

18. See? Threes are important.
19. How long is this film? Two hours, 31 minutes. What's 25% of that total running time? Just about thirty-three minutes. How about that? The screenwriters are right on schedule.

him on his nefarious journey? Yes, it does. Where does it happen? Line 840, which is approximately the 20% mark in the play. It's also the end of Act I. Shakespeare gets a bit of a pass since he's Shakespeare, but even he knows that he can't sustain setup for much longer than a quarter of the story before he has to get into the meat of it.

In script writing, the end of Act I is the reversal that undercuts our understanding of how the world works. It is the point at which the story actually gets moving. Act II is the major portion of the narrative playing out. We have to get all of the pieces we're going to use on the board and into place before we can start the endgame.

In both cases, obstacles and opportunities can be internal and external to the protagonist. Growth and development. Failure and reduction. Pluses and minuses.

Some Opportunities can be used to resolve some of the Obstacles, while some Obstacles will reveal aspects of our protagonist that we will later see as Opportunities.

You do not have to have an equal number of Obstacles and Opportunities. Nor do they have to be matched up.

What are some of the obstacles that confront Hamlet? Let's start with whether or not he is losing his mind. Did he imagine the ghost of his father? Has he just moped about Elsinore long enough that all the damp has broken his brain? It's an awkward series of questions to resolve, but he needs to figure out his mental state before he does something really foolish. And so he monologues, sorts out the answer, and in doing so, affirms that he is resolute in his path.

His Obstacle has been overcome by his willful resolution, and that has now become an Opportunity.

Immediately after he makes the decision to go forward with his terrible plan, he is confronted by Ophelia, who has always doted on the maudlin prince. What does he do? He tries to save her by telling her to fly to a nunnery where she will be safe from the bloody madness that is yet to come.

Ophelia, alas, misunderstands Hamlet's entreaty, suffers a broken heart and kills herself, which creates problems for Hamlet. His Opportunity—the precise understanding of the madness that he must embrace—has created an Obstacle (Ophelia's grief-stricken brother, Laertes) that he must overcome before he can finally confront the murderous King and Queen.

And so on. These pluses and minuses are the "push / pull" of Act II. They are what drive the story forward.

EXERCISE

Give yourself ten to twelve minutes to make some notes in each of these boxes. Give yourself three more if you're feeling extra clever.

Obstacles and Opportunities will play off each other, and the presentation or resolution of one may produce another iteration of the other. Both of which provide means by which you will demonstrate the progress (or lack thereof) toward the goals of both the protagonist and the adversary. You're probably not going to have all the permutations and confabulations sorted out in your head at this point in your outlining process, so it's okay to feel a little frustrated as you try to spend five minutes or so on each of these boxes.

This is normal.

You can iterate more on these when you get into the actual writing or start doing more detailed chapter plotting. Just keep in mind that this portion of the book is the bulk of what actually happens.

You might be inclined to do more or less of each, but bear in mind that our brains yearn for the familiar. We like groups of three, which isn't to say that you can't have less than three Obstacles (and, in fact, you probably will in a short story) or more, but be aware that you're leaving familiar territory. Your story is going to feel unnatural and awkward to your audience without them being consciously aware of what is causing their discomfort.

If you're going to do this, do it consciously, because you are at risk of losing your audience. Make sure you have something else that will hold their attention.

Naturally, working through each iteration of Obstacle or Opportunity can be broken into a series of questions and answers. What is the Obstacle? What happens if the Obstacle can't be resolved? What qualities or items does the Protagonist have that might help resolve the Obstacle? And so on. But don't worry about this now. Let's keep our focus on a higher level.

THE MIRROR

WE'VE FINISHED THE SECOND TIER OF BOXES! IN FACT, we're three-quarters of the way done with this outline. Time to take a moment and pat yourself on the back. And when you're done, let's check in on the structure of our Nine Box Outline Model. We're back to the first column again, which means this is the box where we step back from the actual story and pause for reflection.

We started with the Protagonist.

Then we considered the protagonist's ultimate Goal.

And now we're going to take a few minutes and think about authorial intent. What's your goal in writing this novel?

In keeping with the smart-ass answers that crop up in the first column, someone will pipe up with "I just want to get paid; that's why I'm writing this book." And much like being lazy and stating that the protagonist's goal is only to "survive," this answer might be absolutely true, but that's not the whole reason. And here's why:

No one will buy this book if you flat out tell them that you wrote it merely to get paid.

It's like walking into a job interview and when asked why you want the job, you say, "Eh, it's a paycheck."

The next candidate comes in, and when asked that question, they launch into a passionate answer that lasts nearly five minutes and moves half the room to tears with its earnestness.

Who gets the job? You or the golden-tongued liar? So what if the second candidate was showing up for the interview for the same reason you were. They knew how to lie convincingly.

You're a writer. Lie convincingly, for fuck's sake. Or, better yet, rummage around in that root cellar full of cynical tubers and find some tiny vestigial nubbin of a reason why you wanted to write this book.

There are, after all, less than a dozen plots that work in literature, and hundreds of thousands of books are written every year. Why is yours better than any of the others? How is your book different from all the rest? What are you bringing to the table that the others didn't?

Or, consider this: what's the point of your story? Is it a heartfelt retelling of the perpetual circle of life that pervades existence? Is it a tragic meditation on the finality of death? Is it a weary web of disillusionment or fatalism? Is it about family? Or war? Or how family gatherings are like war, but with smaller weapons? Is it about lost love, or lost honor, or lost keys? Is it optimistic? Pessimistic? Resiliently optimistic?

We're talking theme, here. What is the unifying conceit that underlies the story?

Shortly after I launched my own publishing company, I decided to do an anthology. Now, I'm not a huge fan of themed anthologies, because I find that, as a reader, I typically can't sustain enough enthusiasm about a topic to make it through twenty or thirty stories on that topic. As an editor, who was going to have to read hundreds more stories than those which would end up in the anthology, I feared such an exercise would ruin that theme for me forever. But I had an idea, and it was one I felt had some wiggle room.

The anthology was called *XIII*, and the subtitle was "Stories of Transformation." The call for stories looked like this:

> *"Thirteen" is the first month of a new yearly cycle, wherein the old skins have been shed and the newborns are still learning to walk. "One" and "Three" make "Four," which is the number of completion, of coming home, and of realizing the form that has been in process for some time. Nothing is true; everything is possible. And the more things change, the more they stay the same.*
>
> *The thirteenth Tarot card is Death, and he is the symbol of transformation and rebirth.*
>
> *This is the genesis and root of* XIII.

There are twenty-eight authors in the final anthology, offering twenty-nine stories of transformation. There were almost eight hundred stories submitted during the three months of open call, totaling nearly three million words of fiction. I read them all, and when I settled on the final table of contents, the anthology contained science fiction, mainstream fiction, literary weird, horror, fantasy, comedy, and historical fantasy. It could have been a mess to market. But what tied it all together? A resiliently optimistic belief that transformation bettered us.

If I had plainly stated that in the call for stories, I would have been buried under happy stories of puppies growing wings or ponies getting their magic marks and getting to hang out with the cool equines or something equally diabetic-coma-inducing. In fact, the horror market listings found the call first, and for the first month, I got every single imaginable variant on the serial killer skin-wearing trope. Boy, was I glad when the SF market listings picked the anthology call up.

That story call was the genesis and root of *XIII*, but what grew from that planting was a vision I didn't consciously know when I first had the idea. But I definitely knew what it was by the time I got finished picking stories. There are dozens of anthologies published every year. Why is this one different? Because it is mine, and it reflects my approach to story and theme. It is an extension of who I am and how I see the world.

Tolkien wanted to write something about his experience in the trenches of World War I, and dressed his thoughts up with fantastic creatures and a healthy bit of world-building. *Die Hard* is about Redemption. Jack London wrote stories about man and his eternal conflict with the natural world. *The Hunger Games* is about the power of the individual against tyranny.

Why you write a story can be really simple, and it can be very illuminating. You don't have to tell us all your secrets, but you have to confess a little bit. *Why you, and why this book?*

EXERCISE

Give yourself a few minutes to write down how this book is an extension of who you are and how you see the world. What are you trying to tell your audience through the story of this protagonist, this conflict, and this adversary? What makes you the best person to tell this story in this manner?

This is not the resolution of the book. We'll get to that in a moment. This is the *huzzabuzzawha?* view of the story. The geo-synchronous orbital view of the world you've been building. This is the Demiurge's answer to the question of "Why this world? Why these creatures?" The big picture view.

We'll drill down in a few minutes and get to the macro and micro of this last tier, but for the moment, let's linger up high and speak in the language of theme and intent.

TRANSFORMATION

I'M A BIG FAN OF THE TAROT. THE MORE WILDLY SYMBOLIC the deck, the better. I have at least a dozen decks, and I use them off and on during brainstorming sessions.[20] But for this chapter, I want to direct your attention to two cards of the Major Arcana: the Emperor and the Hanged Man.

The Emperor is the king of the land—the Arthurian figure, if you will. He sits on a throne, holding a scepter and a sphere that symbolize his office, and typically there are other symbolic elements floating around in the background of the card. In many decks, he doesn't sit with both feet planted firmly on the ground; typically, one leg—the right—is canted slightly. In Aleister Crowley's *Thoth* deck, he's actually got his right leg crossed over his left knee.

In contrast, the Hanged Man is inverted from this configuration—upside down, with his hands typically tied behind his back (in Crowley's deck, the Emperor's hands

---

20. They'll come up again later in this book and in Appendix C.

are turned in to his core while the Hanged Man's hands are outstretched). The Hanged Man's right leg is usually crooked behind his left. These two individuals are mirror images of each other: the Emperor is the master of the physical world, and the Hanged Man is the master of no world. He is unrealized potential, the magus waiting for enlightenment.

This symbol of this box in the Nine Box outline model is the inverse of the question mark that we started with in the first box. There we were merely identifying our Protagonist. Now, we need to consider who or what will our Protagonist become?

Unless you're writing episodic narratives, your protagonist will undergo some change during the course of the story. Readers like this. As your Protagonist has suffered various inconveniences imposed by the Adversary (and much worse, even), they are going to learn new things. Some of these things will be revelations about their own character and makeup. Some will be personality aspects of people around them. Some might even be dirty little secrets of our communal history.

All of these will have an impact on the Protagonist. They will cause change, making your protagonist a different individual than when they first entered the story.

EXERCISE

If you've been writing along as you read, you've probably been working the page for an hour or so now, and I'll bet your brain is pretty empty. You don't need to give yourself the same amount of time to work in this box as you did in the beginning.

There's also been some hand-waving[21] going on in the second tier, which can make filling out this box a little tricky. But don't let it get in the way of letting your brain do its fiery magic trick. Just write for three to four minutes. Don't overthink what you put on the page. Right now, we just want to push through to the end.

Who is this person who has emerged from the crucible of your story?

This answer will be influenced by whatever you wrote in the previous box, of course. We're moving from the high level view—the *huzzabuzzawha?*—down to the macro level. We're still not necessarily on the page yet, but we're closing in.

Imagine we're visiting Tim again, the young man from the beginning of this book. We were hovering over a school on a floating island, one that is surrounded by ravenous sharks, and now, we've zoomed in through a window so that we can see the classroom. The second hand on the clock has almost reached the top of the hour. Tim is going to do something when the second hand reaches the twelve, isn't he? We know what it is, but he's not revealed his intentions yet.

---

21. More writer lingo, which is to say "Look over here where I'm waving my hands; pay no attention to *over there*, where I'm madly painting donkeys and gluing plastic horns to their heads for the upcoming unicorn cavalcade scene, which will be *totally* realistic. Trust me."

We're getting very close, though . . .

What change have you wrought over the course of your story? Write it down. Keep it safe.

As an aside, in the J.J. Abrams-directed *Star Trek* reboot of 2009, the screenwriting team of Roberto Orci and Alex Kurtzman pull off a very clever trick. Captain Kirk doesn't change over the course of the story. He's still the same hot-tempered, egocentric, seducer of women that he was in the beginning. However, Starfleet, who have been trying its damnedest to mold him otherwise, suddenly realize that he is exactly the sort of person who they need at that moment to save the universe.

Something to think about when you're considering what change is wrought over the course of your story. In this case, authorial intent (the previous box) influences what changes, which, in turn, is reflected in the final resolution of the narrative (the final box).

THE BOOM BOOM

I'M NOT A VERY GOOD ARTIST, ESPECIALLY WITH A DRY erase marker on a white board. The first few times I tried to draw a representative symbol for this box, I was greeted with lots of confused expressions.

"Is that a sunset?" someone asked.

"No, it's an explosion," someone else decided.

"Maybe, it's a flower," a third person opined.

And that's when I decided each of them was right.

Whatever you see in that box is the final image you want resonating in the mind of your readers. This is the micro view of the *huzzabuzzawha?* (the authorial intent) as viewed through the macro level view (the changes wrought upon the protagonist). How do all of the preceding words of the novel lead us to this last scene, this last page, this last line?

And what do we see there?

This is not the clean-up scene at the end of a novel where you sweep up all the broken pieces and shuffle some of the surviving ones around to ready them for the next outing. This isn't the epilogue where everyone says goodbye (a couple dozen times over, if you're a Hobbit). This is the key moment that brings everything together.

In the *Lord of the Rings*, it's Gollum, capering on the rocky ledge inside Mount Doom. He's got the ring, and he's oblivious to everything else but being reunited with his precious. He doesn't see the edge until it is too late . . .

In *Star Wars*, it's the moment after Luke sinks a pair of torpedoes into the exhaust port on the Death Star. The camera pulls back, and we see the Death Star, hanging in space. The few remaining survivors of the Rebel attack run are flying away. We're outside the Death Star. We have no idea if Luke has really been successful or not. We're on the edge of our seat, waiting. Wondering. And then . . .

Boom.

In *Die Hard*, it's the moment when the expression on Hans Gruber's face changes. You know the one. The shift from sneering criminal mastermind to surprised skydiver.

In *Butch Cassidy and The Sundance Kid*, the scene freezes in this moment as Butch and Sundance charge out of the church.

As writers, we don't have the leisure of the iconic image branding itself on an audience's brain. We have to work a little harder than that. We have to use words and stuff.

After 1,100 pages, Ayn Rand closes *Atlas Shrugged* with "'The road is cleared,' said Galt. 'We are going back to the world.' He raised his hand and over the desolate earth he traced in space the sign of the dollar."

And the last line of *The Lord of the Rings* isn't about Frodo, just to undercut my argument that he is the Protagonist, so thanks for that, J. R. R. Tolkien.

Instead, let's go to Charles Dickens for our own fade-out moment. At the end of *A Tale of Two Cities*, Sydney Carton gets a final speech, and he ends it with "It is a far, far better thing that I do, than I have ever done; it is a far, far better rest that I go to than I have ever known."

Exeunt, as Shakespeare would say.

EXERCISE

For this last box, don't set a timer. Write enough to decide if you've got a sunset, a field of flowers, or an explosion (or something else entirely!). Write some more to solidify this image in your mind.

Put your writing implement down.

Stand up. Pat yourself on the back. Go stick your head out a window and holler at someone. Celebrate a little bit.

After all, you've just brainstormed a novel.

Boom.

MULTI-CHARACTER NARRATIVES

WELL, NOW WHAT? IF YOU'VE BEEN WRITING HARD OVER the last hour or so, you've got a sprawling mess of an outline. Hardly something that you can really sink your teeth into as far as a proper outline goes, isn't it? Guided by this clever Nine Box Outline Model, you've managed to dump a whole bunch of ideas down onto paper. But how are we going to turn all of this into a coherent plan that will get you started?

By doing more writing, of course.

What we've done is break you out of that frozen moment of panic that always rises up with the blank page, and we've discovered that you do, indeed, have a book idea in your head. But the Nine Box model isn't very good at telling you what happens next in the book, and you're going to need to know this in order to actually write the book. So, we're going to take our chaotic outline and stretch it into new shapes. Like balloon animals.

Okay, but what about books with more than one character who is vying to be the main Protagonist? How does this model work for those projects? In short, it doesn't.

The longer answer is that it does—but you need to run through the Nine Box model process for each of them. And then you need to interweave all of their narrative arcs together in a way that is most pleasing and easy to read.

Like I mentioned in a footnote back at the beginning, this is headache-inducing. I feel your pain. I do. But there's no easy way around it.

Each of these character is the Protagonist in their won stories. They've got to have real desires, real goals, and real obstacles to overcome. You're going to have to work through the same process with them as you did for your main character. Otherwise, all of these secondary characters are just walk-on parts—they'll feel and act wooden, and your readers will know.

Oftentimes, these secondary characters can really steal the show, and in a good way. This work isn't soul-sucking drudgery; it's a vital part of building a complicated narrative that will—in the end—draw your readers in more.

Once upon a time, I worked on a collaborative project with six other writers (Erik Bear, Greg Bear, Joseph Brassey, Nicole Galland, Cooper Moo, and Neal Stephenson, in fact). Together, we produced a historical adventure novel *The Mongoliad*. It was originally conceived and produced as an online serial, but was picked up later by Amazon Publishing's SF/F imprint, 47North. They repackaged it as three distinct volumes, and tapped us to write two additional novels (*Katabasis* and *Siege Perilous*), as well as a number of related prequel and ancillary novellas (the *SideQuests*). *The Mongoliad* tells the secret history of the Mongol invasion of Europe in 1241. Some of it is historically accurate (the fighting, most of the bits in Rome); some of it we made up. [22]

We had four storylines going, and each of them had a full complement of characters. From the serial standpoint, tracking the narrative was easy because each story line could be read as a distinct track (how we originally presented it). For the print version, however, I had to figure out how to weave these narratives together in a way that both allowed the arcs to progress naturally and not have them slavishly devoted to ticking off each box in parallel.

It can be done. It's a complicated process, and it will vary a great deal depending on the intricacies and minutia of each storyline. And that's the trick: the storylines need to be worked out as distinct arcs of their own before you combine them.

You almost need chapter-by-chapter outlines. Hmm. I wonder where you could get your hands on some . . . ?

---

22. The core of the idea was that a band of hardened Western knights went all the way to Karakorum in Mongolia to assassinate the Khan of Khans, thereby saving the West. Kind of like *The Dirty Dozen* as a Hong Kong Historical Sword-Fighting novel. Really. That was our elevator pitch for it.

A SUMMARY

OKAY, BEFORE WE GET TO THE NEXT PART, LET'S DO A QUICK recap. The Nine Box Outline Model goes like this: We start with the Protagonist. Who is involved in something that Hooks our attention. Which reveals the Adversary.

These three boxes provide enough framework for the author to articulate the Goal of the Protagonist.

In order to achieve this Goal, the Protagonist suffers a series of Obstacles and Opportunities.

While the Protagonist is jumping through those hoops, the author considers his or her Personal Vision for writing this novel.

Which provides a framework with which to consider the Change the Protagonist undergoes during the course of the novel.

And, ultimately, what has to happen on the page for the author's Personal Goal to be demonstrated via the Change that protagonist undergoes.

Sunset? Field of daisies? Everything goes boom? It all leads to this final resolution.

And there you have it. Nine boxes, filled with lots of words. Of course, it isn't a book yet, and we're going to tackle a number of ways to flesh out all this brainstorming next. After a brief word about that getting stuck . . .

PART TWO

THE
WORDING

STUCKITUDE

Now, let's get this out of the way too: you will get stuck. It may not happen during this brainstorm session, but it might during the long, dark, drag-out period of actually writing the book. The flow has been interrupted. The brain basin where all the ideas are swirling around is empty. The tiny machine that spits out plot coupons has gotten jammed. Whatever metaphor you want to use is fine. You're blocked; you're empty; you're distracted. You know what? You're human. That's all this is telling you.

You've been working hard, and your brain wants a break. Breaks are good. I've taken quite a few while writing this book. I'm going to take a few more before I'm done. Breaks aren't the problem; getting your butt back in the chair is. Finding the rhythm can be almost as difficult as starting with that first blank page.

I hope to subject you to obnoxious writer truisms sparingly, because I realize most of them aren't all that helpful when you're not in the zone, but here's another one: you can write a sentence as readily as you can eat a sandwich.

Now, I don't know about you, but I'm a terribly messy sandwich eater when I'm in the privacy of my own home, where no one can see me dribble mustard down the front of my shirt. I do better in public, because I practice regularly and I've polished my poise and process for when I'm in a fine dining establishment.

Words on the page when you're drafting are practice. Words on the page of a published book are poised and processed.

And to go back to the other truism: a good book is a book that is finished.

All this said, on some days, a little help is appreciated. That's when I turn to some of my secret weapons.

The Tarot, "nuns with guns,"[23] and Brian Eno.

Brian Eno is a musician, producer, artist, and all-around creative thinker. He's been making music for a long time, and some of his records are fabulous for being aural wallpaper when you need a little something to make the writing room feel less like an echo chamber. He and a fellow creative named Peter Schmidt invented *Oblique Strategies*, which are a deck of cards that are meant to give you permission to think outside the box. They're currently in their fifth edition and you can find them online at his website.[24] Elsewhere on the Internet, you can find a history of the cards and their various editions.[25]

---

23. There is actually a terrible Z-grade film called *Nude Nuns with Big Guns*. I've seen the first ten minutes, mainly so that I can report that the title is accurate in its reporting. I don't know what happens in the other 81 minutes. Please don't feel like you need to find out and let me know. It's not a hole that needs filling.

24. http://www.enoshop.co.uk/shop/oblique-strategies.

25. http://www.rtqe.net/ObliqueStrategies/.

Screenwriter John August recently ran a Kickstarter for the the *Writer Emergency Pack*,[26] a deck of twenty-six cards meant to help steer your story back on track.

Kind of like *Oblique Strategies* for writers.

Both *Oblique Strategies* and the *Writer Emergency Pack* have online versions, if you're just looking to get unstuck *right now* and move on. I wouldn't fault you in the slightest. While John and Brian and Peter wouldn't mind your business, they'll also be thrilled to know that their efforts at unsticking creatives everywhere have been helpful.

Card #22 in the *Writer Emergency Pack* is "Zombie Attack," which is not dissimilar to "Nuns With Guns." This is an old gag from the pulp days of writing detective fiction. When in doubt, have someone with a gun show up. Since I tend to have a lot of people with guns in many of my books, another gun wasn't as thought-provoking. Nuns with guns, however, are a different class of complication entirely.

And that's what this tactic is all about. Complicating your narrative in an unexpected way. Sure, it might be completely inappropriate for the genre or story you're telling, but if you stop and consider what would work for your narrative, it might jog things loose.

For instance: *Well, there are no guns in my mid-sixteenth century court drama and there are way too many nuns already, so maybe instead I'll have drunk Venetians with daggers show up. Where did they come from? Why?*

---

26. http://writeremergency.com/

Did someone hire them? Is this a terrible idea and I should just stop being precious about this intimate scene of earnest confession and write the damn thing?

Whatever works, really.

Speaking of which, Tarot cards can be both a blessing and a curse, so approach them appropriately. They are a deck of seventy-eight cards whose origins are somewhat murky, but essentially, they are like traditional playing cards in that they have four suits of fourteen cards each, along with twenty-two extra cards (known as the Major Arcana). During the grand European occult renaissance (which rolled right on through to the early twentieth century), the Tarot became linked with fortune telling, and to this day, they're used extensively for this purpose.

I like them—the Major Arcana, especially—because they're symbolic representation of archetypal qualities and characters. Decks come in all styles and motifs, and there's an entire industry devoted to producing cards across a broad spectrum of art and symbols. If you're interested in using them for writing, I'd recommend buying two or three decks: one that is more traditional in its images (the Rider-Waite or any Marseille variant), one that is more abstract,[27] and one that is keyed more discretely to your project. Lo Scarabeo publishes an impression array of decks, and most of them can be ordered by your local independent bookseller.

---

27. I like the *Liber T* deck, which is based on Crowley's *Thoth* deck, but it strips off some of the built-up occult baggage that weighs down the *Thoth* deck.

What do I do with them? Well, I pull out the Major Arcana and stack them on the table nearby when I'm drafting an outline. If I get stuck, I reach over and draw a card.

The *Thoth* and *Liber T* decks are very rich with color and symbolism, and so if the meaning of the card itself doesn't speak to my stuckitude, then I have other visual clues to work from. Oh, look, there's a winged lion with a flaming sword? How can I work that into this scene?

I also use the Tarot to do readings for my characters once I've gotten the outline done. One of the more well known spreads is the Celtic Cross reading, and we'll walk through how that works a bit later in this section of the book.

Do not fear the stuckitude. It is merely your brain needing to be nudged loose. The techniques herein work for me. They may work for you. You might have better ones. *Caveat emptor* and *Seize the Donkey*, as my wise grandfather used to say.

EIGHTEEN CHAPTERS

So you've got a bunch of ideas now, but what do we do next? Well, how about something actually useful, like a chapter outline? That sounds fantastic. How do we do that?

Grab a fresh sheet of paper, and let's list eighteen chapters. It's a somewhat arbitrary number. It could be twenty-five; it could be sixty-four. It doesn't really matter, but we're going to use eighteen because it makes things look all tidy later. Each chapter will, of course, be between 2,500 and 5,000 words, which means we're totally going to cross that "novel length" threshold.[28]

Now, what we're going to do is quickly write chapter titles for your book. This isn't going to be a drawn-out, thoughtful affair. All we're going to do is slap a structure on this sprawling mass of brainstorming and turn it into a linear series of events that takes us from the beginning to the end. They don't need to reveal everything that

---

28. Anything longer than 40,000 words is considered a novel. Most genres have their own preference as to what the sweet spot is for length. Plan accordingly.

happens in a chapter. They just need to be a bread crumb trail that you can go back to later.

Think of them like the chapter titles in the old boys' and girls' youth detective novels from the last century. "Bob and Doug Find a Clue." "Roger Falls in a Well." "You Damn Kids!" Don't overthink them. Seriously.

Here, let me fill one of them in for you. Chapter 12 will always be "Sex." Chapter 13 will usually be "Things Get Worse." Because that's what happens after sex.

All kidding aside, you'll notice that you run out of steam speed-writing these chapter titles around Chapter 12. "Sex" is as good a title as any, and more often than not, you'll find your characters naturally heading for the bedroom in Chapter 12.[29]

Here's an example. [30]

1. *Simon at the Farm*
2. *Ghost Light*
3. *Hole Haunt*
4. *Driving*
5. *Mining*
6. *Oh No! The Cops*
7. *Friends or Not?*

---

29. Just trust me on this. Chapter 12 is always about sex. It's one of the secrets of writing, in fact.
30. Have I finished this book? Uh . . . look! The Pope! Seriously, though, this was the rundown. The book didn't take, and I set it aside after a couple of tries. The protagonist, Simon, wandered into *Silence of Angels* a year or so later.

8. Spooky
9. Running Through the Night
10. Danger! Danger!
11. Clues
12. Sex
13. Things Get Worse
14. Snatched!
15. Someone Falls in a Hole
16. The Horrible Truth
17. The Conspiracy Revealed
18. Sunset Ride

Without knowing anything about the novel, what can you discern from these chapter titles?

* Chapter 18 is the resolution written for Box 9, isn't it?

* Chapter 1 introduces of the Protagonist (Box 1).

* Chapter 2 is filled with interesting things (Box 2).

* Chapter 3 is our first glimpse of the Adversary (Box 3).

* Chapters 4 and 5 are where the author is figuring out the Protagonist's goal (Box 4).

* Chapters 6, 10, and 14 are a bunch of Obstacles (Box 5).

* Chapters 7, 11, and 13 are Opportunities (Box 6).

* Chapter 15 is the dark night of the soul in the book. The protagonist must face all the crap that has happened and decide if they're going to step up and finish the book.

* Therefore, Chapter 16 & 17 are the revelation of the decisions made about Authorial Intent (Box 7) and the Protagonist's transformation (Box 8).

Every outline will have some variation to it. As you can
see, however, there will be crossover between what you
wrote in the boxes and the chapter titles for the book.
In fact, let's go one step further and apply the cinematic
three-act structure to these eighteen chapters. Wherein
we'll get something that looks this chart:

Chapter	Box	Act
1	BOX 1	ACT 1
2	BOX 2	ACT 1
3	BOX 2	ACT 1
4	BOX 3	ACT 2
5	BOX 3	ACT 2
6	BOX 4	ACT 2
7	BOX 4	ACT 2
8	BOX 5	ACT 2
9	BOX 5	ACT 2
10	BOX 5	ACT 2
11	BOX 6	ACT 2
12	BOX 6	ACT 2
13	BOX 6	ACT 2
14	BOX 7	ACT 2
15	BOX 7	ACT 2
16	BOX 8	ACT 3
17	BOX 8	ACT 3
18	BOX 9	ACT 3

As with all models, take them with a grain of salt. They're based on hundreds and hundreds of examples. There will always be outliers that challenge the model. Some of them will work; some of them won't. You don't have to be the writer that breaks all convention. You can be the writer who hits their marks and quietly cashes the check and goes home at the end of the day. Be aware of the models because if you're struggling with your book and something feels off in it, my first guess is that you're out of true with the models.

If you take four chapters to introduce your Protagonist, your audience will say the book drags and it never caught their attention.

If you introduce the Adversary first and dig into the obstacles immediately after, your audience will find themselves adrift, unable to figure out whom they should be rooting for.

Can you imagine Ayn Rand beginning *Atlas Shrugged* with having John Galt answer the question she posed in the first line with his ninety-page speech from the middle of the novel (which is the author having a character deliver an inordinately lengthy monologue that is a thinly veiled diatribe articulating the authorial intent)?

When a story opens with an exciting action sequence that seems to be the final moments of the Protagonist and then inserts a title card that basically says "X days/hours/ minutes earlier," what is that story missing? A reasonably interesting answer to the Hook of Box 2. They've just substituted a sequence from later in the book (one of the final Obstacles, perhaps). Why doesn't that work? Because, within the context of the narrative arc, the Protagonist has already gone through most the change they are going to undergo in the course of the novel, and we haven't even met them yet. How can we track the Protagonist's change, if we have to back up and pretend we don't know it?

Know the models. Know the narrative rhythms that we all unconsciously find comforting. It's an annoying truism that you can break rules once you know what they are. In this case, be aware of how breaking them is going to affect your audience's engagement with the material. Break them, if you will, but do so consciously.

And have something clever up your sleeve to hide what you just did.

THE MASTER FORMULA

You've been waiting pages and pages for this, haven't you? The ultimate secrets that will make book writing as simple as baking a cake.

Well, it's not quite as simple as that. Almost. But not quite.

There is, actually, something known as the Master Formula. Shhh! Here it is . . .

Back in the early part of the twentieth century, Lester Dent was one of the go-to guys for pulp fiction. He wrote a great number of the *Doc Savage* novels, and as a guide to writing them, he developed a Master Formula. It's presented as if you were breaking down a 6,000 word story, but it can be readily applied to the structure of a novel as well. You can find the entirety of the Master Formula at paper-dragon.com.[31] It's worth taking a look at as you dig deeper into the page-by-page breakdown of your story.

But for our needs right now, I'll let English writer Michael Moorcock—who wrote his share of pulp novels in three to five days—sum up Dent's formula:

---

31. http://www.paper-dragon.com/1939/dent.html

First, he says, split your six-thousand-word story up into four 1,500 words parts. Part one, hit your hero with a heap of trouble. Part two, double it. Part three, put him in so much trouble there's no way he could possibly get out of it.[32]

Wait a second. That just sounds like "things get worse" over and over again. There's got to be more to it than that. Ah, but what about the final part?

Moorcock summarizes the whole structure in two sentences.

All your main characters have to be in the first third. All your main themes and everything else has to be established in the first third, developed in the second third, and resolved in the last third.

Hang on . . . This sounds suspiciously like the three-act structure we've been using. The first part corresponds to Act 1, the second and third part—things get worse and worse—are Act 2, and we wrap it all up in Act 3.

It can't be that easy, can it?

It almost is. But not quite.

If that seems too cleverly reductive, then let's consider another way to frame your narrative that is a bit more complicated . . .

---

32. This is taken from a fantastic conversation that Moorcock has with Colin Greenland in *Michael Moorcock: Death is No Obstacle* (Savoy, 1992). This quote and the following quote appear on page 17.

THE MYTH OF THE MYTH

HOLLYWOOD LIKES TO PRETEND WRITERS DON'T EXIST, BUT scripts don't write themselves.[33] Books don't write themselves either, and even though pundits like to proclaim the death of literature (as do some literary critics), people are still reading. They like stories. They always have. They always will. A good story will always find a place at a table, and if you go back far enough in any society's history, you'll find their origins, delivered as story.

Joseph Campbell gets a lot of grief about getting all reductionist on the vast wealth of the cultural mythologies throughout the world, but what his seminal book, *The Hero With a Thousand Faces*, did was enumerate the fundamental similarities among many of these disparate stories. It was never a lesson in "this is the one true way to tell a story." Rather, Campbell was taking stock and recognizing that many of the stories of the human condition follow a common arc, regardless of language or locale or cultural make-up. The arc of the hero—the protagonist in our story—has a distinct shape.

---

33. Nor do committees, but that's another diatribe for another time.

As writers, it is important for us to know the natural rhythm of a story because this is what makes our audiences get that warm, tingling feeling in their bellies. It's what is going to make them show up again and again for more stories. Long-running television shows or book series don't run long because they're constantly changing their shape. They run long because they are comfortable in their familiarity.

Recently, a bestselling suspense writer offered the statistic that a vast majority of the American reading public only buys two books a year, and one of those books is bought in an airport bookstore.[34] I was, at the time I read this bit of data, reading both this author's first book and his current book (somewhere near the two-dozen mark in the series), and one of the noticeable differences in the author's style between those two books was the lack of words on the page in the current book. And it occurred to me that most flights are three to four hours long, and if you're buying a book in an airport, you're looking for something to entertain you for only three to four hours.

Familiarity does not breed contempt. Familiarity breeds an open wallet.

Know the rhythms of story. Know the traditional structures. They will guide you, especially when you're in

---

34. I'm not going to cite the conversation because the author didn't explicitly offer his source for this data, because if it is true, then it means that you and I and all our friends are doing a lot to sway the statistics every time we buy a book somewhere else. Like, you know, daily. Which is groovy of us, but it still makes me sad. The validity of this data point is also outside the scope of my anecdote so just roll with it, okay?

the early stages of planning a narrative arc. You can go off-structure later, but do it when you know where you want to go and why. We all hate the axiom of "Know the rules before you break them" because it means that we have to follow the rules first, and following the rules is always a pain in the ass, right? How many of you read all the instructions that come with your new electronic gizmo before you start using it?[35]

Uh huh. That's what I thought.

Anyway, Campbell gave us a simple chart that breaks down the natural rhythm of a narrative arc. It doesn't work for every story that you might want to tell, but it will work for a vast majority of them. If your book feels like you're trying to shove a Spandex body stocking onto an over-weight, gassy goat, it's probably because you're trying to be clever and dress the goat from the back end first. And that's just the wrong way to dress a goat.

The Hero's Journey is cyclical. In the simplest description, it is the story of a protagonist who must leave their safe and predictable life and embark upon a perilous journey. The journey takes them to a world unlike the one they know, and upon their return, they have been transformed by their journey, which allows them to return to their normal lives, but with one difference.

Usually a pretty big one.

---

35. Notice how most gizmos don't even come with instructions any more. They come with tips and help files and other things that get in the way of using the gizmo for a period of time. Because that's the only way you'll bother to pay attention to the instructions for the gizmo's feature set.

The chart we're building lists of Campbell's various stages of the Hero's Journey, and it's a rare story that actually hits every single stage.[36] I've listed them all merely to give you a number of places where you can hook in your narrative. Not every story has to have a Meeting with the Goddess, a trial of Woman as Temptress, a little Atonement with the Father, AND some Apotheosis. Unless you're working on a doorstopper of an epic coming-of-age fantasy sequence that spans eighteen volumes, in which case, each of those is a single volume. More likely, your story will have a confrontation between the protagonist and some aspect of themselves in the alternate world, typically either a confrontation with the familial figure opposite them or a reconciliation with that familial guide whom they have been seeking.

In *Star Wars*, for instance, we can read Vader killing Ben Kenobi as a removal of the possibility of atonement with the Father (Ben, who was a surrogate father for Luke), which galvanizes Luke to embrace his destiny (enlightened ghost Ben even tells him as much later on). Or the scene can be read as Ben sacrificing himself to Vader in order to show Luke the true power of the Force, which is an apotheosis of the magi figure that allows the protagonist

36. There are a number of books out there that distill the Hero's Journey down to various prompts and life-affirming examples, but really, if you're interested in the minutia of Campbell's research, just go get a copy of *The Hero With a Thousand Faces*. Yes, it can get dense in its minutia, but Campbell came back to the book several times during his career, and his final edition in 2008 does some nice summary work that is invaluable to the writer brain.

to see the path they must take in order to realize their full potential. Or, Vader—who is Luke's actual father—kills the false father, Ben Kenobi, in an attempt to reconcile himself with his absent son. You can read it any number of ways, but the actual action of that scene remains the same.[37]

And not all protagonists pass through all the stages in the same fashion. For instance, while Luke laments that he'll never get off the rock that is Tatooine (and doesn't, in fact, until he is spirited away by the wise magi, Ben Kenobi), which is representative of the "refusal of the call" stage, in *The Hunger Games*, Katniss Everdeen volunteers for the games to protect her sister. Her "call to adventure" is a threat against her family, and she bypasses the "refusal of the call" altogether.

Many of the myths that Campbell investigated are patriarchal in design, and the protagonist is typically male. It doesn't mean that all narrative is bound to this structure. Campbell was outlining a specific type of narrative structure found throughout different cultures, and understandably, in an effort to buttress his thesis, his emphasis was on data that supported the conclusion he was seeking.

---

37. Now, I'll bet that Lucas didn't know that Vader was Luke's father at the time *Star Wars* was written and filmed, but the fact that the revelation at the end of Empire doesn't negate the power of Kenobi's death scene speaks to the effectiveness of the underlying mythological arc that Lucas clung to for *Star Wars*. In fact, knowing the true lineage between the characters actually makes that scene in *Star Wars* work more effectively because of how it fits into the mythological structure, and why the sequence in *The Empire Strikes Back* where Luke confronts the phantasm of his father on Dagobah and fails is a secondary repetition of the protagonist's cycle through this journey.

The structural nature of the Hero's Journey—as well as the cultural foundations these myths supported—was based on the fact that the role of protector and hero was a male role. The shape of the narrative arc is defined by the traditional male role in society, but that does not negate the entirety of the mythological structure for women—especially women in a modern society that does not have the same strictly defined roles for men and women.

And these differences also shape the protagonist's arcs. There's an underlying whiff of revenge in Luke's arc (the Empire did kill his adopted parents, after all), and because violence has been done to him, he is allowed do violence in return. Katniss, on the other hand, is protecting her family, who have been threatened with violence. Her refusal, if she has one, is her reluctance to do violence to others, until it is absolutely necessary.[38] It can be argued that her use of violence is driven by revenge as well, but ask yourself: did Luke ever pass up the opportunity to kill a stormtrooper when he had the chance?

Once the protagonist leaves the safety of their home (the world they knew), they must journey to a gate where they must face a gatekeeper. Once they pass the gate, they enter a sacred space where the rules of the normal world are suspended.[39] Various adventures occur here, culminat-

---

38. Notice that during the first game, she becomes the mother figure to Rue, signifying her own transformation from child to woman. This is her Meeting with the Goddess moment, and she does not need the other stages to accomplish her goal.

39. Mircea Eliade calls this "sacred" space in contrast with the "profane" space of the normal world (cf., *The Sacred and The Profane*).

ing in an event that transforms the hero, whereupon the journey back home begins. If we imagine the cycle as a circle, it might look something like the following:

Notice how the crossing of the gate into the sacred world and the return to profane space coincide with the separation between acts?

Act I defines the world of the narrative for us, and the break between Act I and Act II is a change in the world as it has been defined. It's not merely an awareness of the threat that faces the protagonist and their world; it is a shift into the unknown. In *The Hunger Games*, it happens in that moment when Katniss steps into the arena where the games are fought. In *Star Wars*, it happens when Han Solo triggers the hyperdrive and the stars get all streaky and the Millennium Falcon vanishes from the screen.

You will get some compression of the journey once the hero has been transformed. It's like getting a bonus coupon for leveling up. Once the hero has received the boon they sought to receive in sacred space, they are afforded certain privileges on their return. Cynically, we can look upon these privileges as narrative short-hand. While the journey to the nadir of the circle is well-documented as the series of obstacles and opportunities that test and refine the character of the protagonist, the return is shortened for several reasons. Primarily, the protagonist has received their boon and/or been enlightened, and there is no longer a need to document their struggle because the bulk of their struggle (which has been a quest for identity as well) is over. What remains is merely an application of their newfound knowledge to the greater crisis facing their profane world.

And secondly, your audience has been patient. Once they know the hero has the goods, they want to see the ultimate showdown. As writers, it's best not to make them wait too long.

This is why the eagles show up really late in *The Lord of the Rings*. It's not until Frodo and Sam have gone through the crucible and been reformed that they are allowed to use their Post-Transformation Voucher.[40] Yes, the book would have been much shorter if the eagles had just come and picked everyone up at Rivendell back in the beginning,

---

40. Frodo has lost everything but the Ring during his passage through Cirith Ungol and the lair of Shelob, right? He's basically naked on the plain of fire.

but the heroes had not suffered through their journey into the mythic space yet. You don't get the coupon without singeing some hair and losing a pair of pants or two. But, once you get your Post-Transformation Voucher, then yes, it's straight to the top of the queue for you.

The hero—transformed, enlightened, recipient of the boon of the Goddess—returns to their home, and in some climatic encounter, vanquishes the Adversary, thereby saving their community. Huzzah!

Note that it is not uncommon for the hero to then leave their community. Not because they've seen the world and are now bored with the mundanity of living at home again, but because they have been transformed. If they have done violence during the course of their journey, then they are marked with that blood. They are, in some ways, dangerous to their community. They cannot stay because they imperil the innocents.[41]

EXERCISE

Draw a circle on the page beneath your chart. Quarter it like the illustration earlier in this chapter. Write the chapter number that represents that break between the Acts (at ninety degree increments). Put hash marks along the circle for the remaining chapters. Working clockwise around your circle, write the words "WANT," "GET,"

---

41. See William Munny in Clint Eastwood's *Unforgiven*. He constantly warns the kid of the dangers of hiring a killer, and sure enough, things get out of hand.

"NEED," and "USE" in each quadrant. Consider how these words reflect the course of the narrative in each section. Notice the subtle distinctions between "WANT" and "NEED" and "GET" and "USE," and how each pair is opposite each other on the circle. "WANT" is in profane space; "NEED" is in sacred space. Both are emotional drivers for the story. "GET" and "USE" are applications of the prior sections' emotional impetus.

TAROT CARDS

I AM, IF IT ISN'T ALREADY ABUNDANTLY CLEAR, A PANTSER. I do draw up outlines, and I do a lot of thinking (but probably not enough planning), but over the years, I've come to realize that if I overplan a book, then all of the magic goes out of the writing for me. I'm not excited about what's going onto the page, and my boredom translates right to the reader. Therefore, I write to be amazed by what the characters want to do, which is a dangerous way to write. The creative process can wiggle about in awkward ways as you and the characters wrestle with the story, though once everyone gets on the same page, the work happens quickly.

One of the ways I plan is to feed my subconscious, and I do that with Tarot cards.

The subconscious brain is really good at untangling knots and figuring out pathways through mazes—especially when you're not paying attention to it. Your brain is always working on some issue with the book, whether you're aware of it or not, and when it has a problem solved, it'll shove the solution into your conscious mind.

To that end, tarot cards are great for jamming a bunch of archetypal symbols and concepts into your subconscious brain, which will happily chew on them as it darts through the labyrinthian construct you're building. It's a trap to think of the cards as literal representations of the various aspects of the story. Once they are laid out before you, it is up to you to provide the narrative. In doing so, I've found that I've had to articulate aspects of the story that I hadn't otherwise been conscious of. I find new pathways through the narrative that have been suggested by the cards (and amplified by my subconscious).

And if you throw down a spread, and it makes absolutely no sense in regard to your plot or your characters, by all means, pick the cards up and try again. The cards can't force a structure contrary to the writer's desire. They work with you because they are reflective, all the way down to the deepest part of your dreaming brain.

I always bring a deck of tarot cards to a workshop, and I tell the class that I'll draw a card for anyone who gets stuck during the exercises. Typically, the class is skeptical of this sort of madness. However, more often than not, every card drawn is a surprise and a revelation to the writer. It's a lot of fun to watch their faces light up as if I'm doing some fabulous magic trick by providing them the exact visual cue they needed in order to cut through the knot they had been fighting.

The cards aren't magic. It's our ability to instinctively see patterns and create narrative that is, because we like to see patterns, after all.

There are many ways to do a reading with the tarot, but I have found that the Celtic Cross style of reading matches up nicely with the chart we're building for our book. Before you start the reading, focus your mind on a question you want some insight into—or, in the case of our outline, a narrative arc for a protagonist. The tarot deck is divided into two major portions: the Minor Arcana, suit cards; and the Major Arcana, twenty-two cards that are larger archetypes. I tend to do these readings using only the Major Arcana cards, because I find their meaning and symbolisms speak more directly to the thematic arc. The Minor Arcana are fine, but they tend to reference elements and events on a smaller scale.[42]

Once we lay out ten cards in a pattern that resembles a cross and a staff (see following page), let's consider it as a model for our Protagonist: who is this person, what lies behind them, what supports them, what weighs on their mind, and so on.

The staff on the right is a rising line indicative of what lies before the Protagonist—their goals, their future, their obstacles, and so on.

42. Compare the Six of Swords which means "a regretful but necessary transition" and The Tower, which depicts a bolt of lightning striking a tower and hurling a couple of crown-wearing unfortunates into the void. The former sounds like a minor inconvenience; the latter is an "OMG! We're all going to die!" sort of event. One of these is going to be more useful to you as a narrative suggestion. Naturally, when you use the cards a lot, it may seem like you're not getting enough variation with just twenty-two cards, but that only means you need to dig deeper into the symbolism suggested by the card. Much like the argument that there are only six plots and the rest is how you approach the story that makes it unique, how you interpret the cards is entirely subjective and part of your magic.

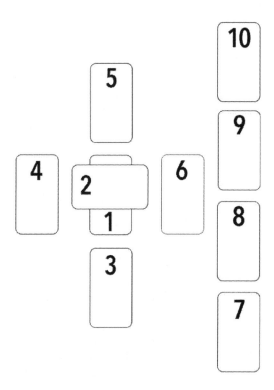

Looks familiar, doesn't it?

1. THE HEART OF THE MATTER.

This card represents the protagonist. It can be a literal representation. It can be an occupational representation. This is how the author refers to the protagonist. It may not strictly be their job or their identity. For instance, any character played by Will Ferrell in a film could readily be represented by The Fool card, and what changes from film to film is merely the character's occupation and situation. We'll still think of him as a bumbling well-meaning idiot, or, like we see in many decks, the buffoon who is unaware that he's about to walk off a cliff or that a dog wants to snack on his nutsack.

2. THE OPPOSING FACTOR.

This is the complicating factor that disguises or otherwise obscures the Heart (which is why it is laid at a ninety degree angle across the first card). Think of this card as the Adversary, aka "that which opposes the protagonist." In narratives that force that protagonist to deal with the natural world (any Jack London story, for instance), the opposition comes from the natural world.

In *San Andreas*, one of the most recent natural disaster morality films, Dwayne Johnson AKA The Rock is opposed by a great earthquake that tries to drop the grand state of California into the Pacific Ocean. Characters who get in his way certainly qualify as antagonists, but they are more properly categorized as either agents of the Adversary or as obstacles that our heroic protagonist must overcome in order to win against the Adversary.

Some Tarot cards don't explicitly represent people. For instance, it can be hard to look at The Moon, which represents the divine creative madness that either liberates or destroys, and immediately think, "Oh, yes, this is

Biff, the protagonist's childhood nemesis who has gone on to become a megalomaniacal industrialist who has never forgotten (or forgiven) that wedgie the protagonist gave him during gym one day in high school, and now, twenty years later, has built an entire chemical weapons manufacturing empire just so that he can dose the water supply of the small town where the protagonist lives merely for petty REVENGE!"[43]

Don't worry some much about the literal interpretation of the card, and let a more symbolic apsect of the card suggest the nature of the Adversary to you. Ask and answer the question of why does this card oppose the protagonist?

3. THE ROOTS.

There is a foundation beneath the protagonist, even if they have been shoved out of their comfort zone. Who were they? Where did they come from? Who supported them in the past and why? Now, you'll notice that both this card and the next don't show up on our chart, and the reason for that is because they are part of our protagonist's backstory. They are what lies beneath and behind the protagonist. Motivation, perhaps. Deep secrets, most likely. Character depth, most assuredly.

---

43. It only seems petty to the protagonist, of course. For Biff, this has been an all-consuming fixation for many, many years, and the protagonist's seeming unawareness of Biff's long-standing rage and embarrassment only increases how horrifically everyone the protagonist ever loved is going to die after drinking the tainted water. Especially the innocent children of the orphanage where Biff works.

4. THE PAST.

That which is immediately behind the protagonist. As noted above, this card isn't on the chart because it is behind the protagonist. Now, backfill isn't evil, but it can only happen on the page when it is there servicing the narrative. Your readers aren't going to care about a huge chunk of backstory if they don't know anything about who the protagonist is and what they are doing. Ground them first, and then give them more texture.

Richard Stark wrote a series of books about a thief named Parker. One of the clever things he did was that he set the narrative viewpoint as third party limited whenever Parker was the focus of the story. We never get to know what goes on Parker's head, which means his backstory is always hidden from us.

At the beginning of the first book, *The Hunter*, Parker is walking across the George Washington Bridge into New York City. We see that he's a bastard and that he's on a mission, but we don't know why. Stark keeps the narrative moving forward—Parker gets to the city, Parker reinvents himself, Parker finds Lynn (his ex-wife), he threatens her about the whereabouts of someone named Mal—without giving the audience a chance to really ground themselves. And it's not until we learn about the existence of Mal that Stark takes a break and gives us enough backstory to make us happy.

Contrast this with the 1967 movie version called *Point Blank*, which begins with ten minutes of incomprehensibly chaotic backstory shoved at the viewers while "Walker" lies in a jail cell in Alcatraz.[44] By the time we get to the walking across the bridge scene (rendered in the film as Marvin's character walking through LAX), we've been given all of the backstory that Stark keeps from us, and the problem with this version is that we've been confused by too many disconnected elements and the fact that Walker comes across as a drunk rube who gets taken advantage of by both Mal and some dude who apparently works for the FBI when he's not riding the tour boat across San Francisco Bay.

In *The Hunter*, we know there is history to these characters, and it informs how and why they interact in the narrative arc of the novel, but we don't see it until we need it.

Kurt Vonnegut once offered eight rules of writing. The eighth rule says: "Give your readers as much information as possible as soon as possible."

I have a caveat: "Give this information only when the readers are ready to understand what it means."

Stark strings us along for two chapters before he gives us any of this history, and he knows that he's testing our patience, which is why the book cooks right along until

---

44. One of John Boorman's first features, and a major starring role for Lee Marvin. Too bad it's also part of the brightly lit New Wave period of noir in film. I blame Godard and the Dave Clark 5.

Also, why the filmmakers had to call Parker "Walker" is beyond me. The same is true for *Payback*, the Mel Gibson version, where the protagonist is "Porter." It's like some studio exec somewhere laid down a mandate that the studio was doing their own version (even though they gave Stark a "Based on" credit). In which case, the name had to be different, like "Horker" or "Tucker" or some other nonsense. Hollywood is weird.

that point. We'll give him some leeway, but eventually we want some backstory, and just before we're about to lose our patience with him, he gives us what we want. And we're eager for it because we know we need it![45]

5. THE ALTERNATE FUTURE (AKA THE VISION).

This is the future the protagonist seeks—their goal, their idealized realized state of being. Who they want to be, if you will, but it can also be read as the world they want to live in.

This is the vision that drives the protagonist to step out of their normal—read safe—world and embark upon their journey. They want something, which forces them to make a change (or the change is forced upon them, in which case what they want may very well be a means or tool that will allow them to return to their preferred state of rest).

"As above, so below" is an old alchemical saying that is the key to the mystical transformation of both metals and men, meaning that transformations in both metaphysical and spiritual states can (and should) be mirrored in

---

45. *Point Blank* makes us watch Lee Marvin hang out at Alcatraz (which is abandoned at this time) while he magically heals from several gunshot wounds. All the while, we're scratching our heads and wondering why he's hanging off the barbed wire fence like's just some dude catching rays. Contrast again with *Payback*, Brian Helgeland's studio-mangled remake. The studio slapped a voice-over driven intro that basically boils down *Point Blank*'s extended opening to about a minute and a half. The voice-over totally puts us in protagonist's head, but it also immediately grounds us, which is good because we've paid $10 for the seat and another $10 for a tub of popcorn, and we're not sitting in the dark theater to be confused by a narrative we have to think through.

physical states as well. The card above the protagonist and the card below the protagonist (3: THE ROOT) are tied together in that the protagonist is supported by one as they reach for the other. Or that influences in one mirror change in the other. There is a cyclical structure to the protagonist's life that circles down from the VISION to the HEART to the ROOT to the HEART to the VISION again, and each state change carries with it influence from the card it has just passed through.

This is seen in the old vegetation cult rituals where a young man is elevated to being "king" of the tribe. After a year, he is removed from office (typically sacrificed—in a manner just as you might expect), the tribe goes through a period of mourning, and then a new king is elected, returning the tribe to the elevated VISION state again.

6. THE IMMEDIATE FUTURE.

That which is right in front of the protagonist. While the previous five cards inform who the protagonist is, our attention is drawn to what is happening RIGHT NOW.

In the narrative structure, this is mapped to the events at the opening of the book. In any Clive Cussler novel (or James Bond film, for that matter), we are always treated to a short sequence wherein our protagonist (Dirk Pirk or James Bond) is in the midst of some dangerous assignment (though, in Dirk's case, more often than not, he's just out diving for treasure when nefarious hirelings start shooting at him). This is typically the "before credits" sequence in a film where our attention becomes transfixed by what is going on, and it may very well play into the larger narrative arc that is the full story, but it is a stand-alone sequence that exists mainly to introduce us to the world and the protagonist.

If we look at the physical layout of the cards on the table, there is a straight line from the protagonist's past to his identity (obscured slightly by the adversary) to the immediate future. Think of Parker walking across the George Washington Bridge. He's moving in a straight line, walking from the past to the future, his eyes on his destination. This is how we approach the opening of the narrative: a straight line to the immediate future with our protagonist.

7. THE MIRROR.

This is typically representative of how the querent sees themselves: their identity, when everything is stripped away.

For the author, this drifts outside the direct scope of the narrative, in a way. Regardless of whether we explicitly reveal who the protagonist truly is, we have to give our readers some measure of this revelation, and how much we want to give them and in what manner we want to reveal this secret about our protagonist speaks to how we're going to approach the book. Stark wanted to explore the anti-hero with Parker, but he didn't want to get lost in the psychology of the "villain," so he kept us removed from Parker. But that doesn't stop us from knowing *who* Parker is. We just don't know the *why*, but that's the story that Stark wanted to tell.

So, while the MIRROR is representative of the protagonist, it is also a reflection of us as the writer.

8. THE EYE.

How the outsider world perceives the protagonist.

Here's part of the overarching conflict of the narrative: who the protagonist thinks they are and how they are perceived by the rest the world are not in sync. It is this disconnect that forces the protagonist out of their comfort zone, sending them off on the narrative.

Additionally, how they are going to deal with this external perception informs both their internal narrative arc (see the MIRROR above) and their external arc.

This card reflects a significant portion of the second act—dealing with this dichotomy of perception versus reality (however subjective that may be). And isn't that always the case with figuring out how to make the rest of the world see us as we really are? Your poor characters are no different. Always misunderstood.

9. THE GUIDE.

The guide shows us the path that leads from the HEART to the MIRROR, through the VISION and the EYE. While the narrative moves—more or less—in a straight line, this "path" is the course through the series of obstacles and opportunities that confront the protagonist over the course of the narrative. How Byzantine is the route through all the complications? Does the protagonist lose their way? Is there a fruit stand along the route that offers a tantalizing lure?

For Parker, in *The Hunter*, it was the simplest of paths: he simply kept going to the next guy up the food chain within the Outfit, explaining how Mal owed him money, and since Mal gave that money to the Outfit, the Outfit now owed Parker. The Outfit didn't quite see it that way, and therein lies the central conflict of the novel.

Now, *Game of Thrones* or *War or Peace* are a little more complicated . . .

10. THE OUTCOME.

Regardless of who the protagonist thinks they are or who they think they are going to become, there is an ultimate transformation or resolution to their journey, which is represented by this final card. Does the author respect the protagonist's wishes and realize their VISION or is the final scene in the novel a different resolution entirely? What is the authorial intent in this ending? How does that change our understanding of the protagonist's journey?

In most serial narratives, the characters reset themselves at the end of the novel. They may change or grow over the course of the arc, but they remain fundamentally the same, and this is the natural inclination of such fiction. The lesson imparted though the narrative arc is meant for the reader and not necessarily for the protagonist.[46]

---

46. Fortunately, we've moved past needing those final moments where everyone sits around and gabs about the After School Special moment that's been loaded into the final act of the narrative. Whew.

EXERCISE

You know how this works. Grab a deck. Lay out the cards. Walk through the commentary above as you analyze each card in reference to your outline. Scribble notes that reference each card in the respective area of your chart.

Again, and I really want to stress this, if all of this seems like mystical bullshit, skip it. Doing a reading like this—at this stage in the planning process—is not a substitute for knowing your narrative arc. It is meant to amplify what you already have in mind. The cards merely remind you that your subconscious has your back. This is a tool that you can reference later when you get caught in the Dark Well of Despair—a knotted rope, if you will, that you can used to climb out of the well.

CHAPTER	BOX	3-ACT	LESTER DENT	CAMPBELL	TAROT
1	BOX 1	ACT 1		The Call to Adventure	THE HEART
2	BOX 2	ACT 1	Heap of Trouble	Refusal of the Call	THE IMMEDIATE FUTURE
3				Supernatural Aid	
4	BOX 3			The Crossing of the First Threshold	THE OPPOSING FACTOR
5			More Trouble	The Belly of the Whale	
6	BOX 4			The Road of Trials	THE VISION
7				Meeting the Goddess	
8	BOX 5	ACT 2		Woman as Temptress	THE GUIDE
9				Atonement with the Father	
10			Still More Trouble	Apotheosis	
11	BOX 6			The Ultimate Boon	
12				Refusal of Return	
13				The Magic Flight	
14	BOX 7			Rescue from Without	THE MIRROR
15				Crossing the Return Threshold	
16	BOX 8	ACT 3	Resolution	Master of Two Worlds	THE EYE
17				Freedom to Live	
18	BOX 9				THE OUTCOME

CONCLUSION

AND HERE WE ARE, AT THE END. WHAT SORT OF ENDING is it? We've raced through a brain-filling process and challenged ourselves to set aside the panic of the first page and write. If you did the exercises for each box and then applied all the various models to your story, you've got a really solid start to a novel. You know what happens next, don't you? Right?

More writing.

But look at what you've done already. You can't say you don't have an idea anymore. You can't tell me that you're not a good idea person or that you don't know where to start.

It's all right there. Chapter one, page one is what? The first box. What's in the first box?

Go, tell your story.

The rest of this is book is filled with extra material for you to explore at your leisure.

Appendix A is a list of books that I've found useful over the years. Some of them are writing books. Some of them are not. All creative processes, regardless of medium, are useful, and I like looking a little farther afield to see what other disciplines are doing when it comes to focusing their creative energies.

Appendix B is a Case Study for *Die Hard*.

I figured that I might as well map the whole film to this model just as an exercise for readers to see how it works. Yes, I know that I'm tying a novel process to a film. I'm both visual and lazy. Besides I think it is easier to see what we've discussed in this book in a cinematic format. Plus it is easier for everyone to watch the same version of the film, unlike asking you to track down the specific edition of a book so that my page numbers matched with yours.

Finally, **Appendix C** is a demonstration of how I use the Tarot to generate a quick narrative arc. It's all smoke and mirrors, really, but as an exercise in brainstorming, it always makes me think outside the various boxes that I've just stuffed a bunch of ideas into.

Finally, one of the last activities I do when I'm all done with the exercises outlined in this book is that I go write out the movie trailer for the novel. I do this for a few reasons. I find the screenplay format to be utterly foreign to the way novels are written, and for that reason, I have to think differently. It also allows for commentary to the director and actors as to how people, places, and events are to be visualized. These notes are the sort of shorthand that would never appear in the book itself, but they are the sort of notes that I have floating around my head after spending an hour or two brainstorming.

The movie trailer is a visual and emotional teaser for the story. All the box filling and chapter outlining can sometimes be very dry and methodical. The trailer gives you a chance to offer an impression of the book. What does it look like? How does it make you feel?

Good movie trailers evoke a mood more than reveal anything concrete about the film. Look at the trailers for *Mad Max: Fury Road* or David Fincher's version of *The Girl With The Dragon Tattoo*. Do they tell you anything about the story? Do they smack you in the face with an impression of what your experience of the story is going to be like? Watch how they evoke entirely different worlds and moods.

I believe that creating story is a powerful gift that, so often, is done in a near vacuum. It's hard work, and it may never pay back the time and effort you put into it.

But you're going to do it anyway, aren't you?

I know. Me too.

There will always been a need for more stories. Hopefully, this material helps bring you closer to your goal of being a professionally well-paid writer, and I wish you—each and every one of you—the best of luck as you follow your path to publication.

"Let the world burn through you. Throw the prism light, white hot, on paper."
—Ray Bradbury

APPENDIX A:
EXTRA READING

Writing and the Creative Process

Arias, Martín and Martín Hadis, *Professor Borges: A Course on English Literature* (New Directions, 2013).

Bradbury, Ray, *Zen in the Art of Writing* (Bantam, 1992).

Cook, William Wallace, *Plotto: The Master Book of All Plots* (Tin House Books, 2011).

Delany, Samuel R., *About Writing* (Wesleyan University Press, 2005).

Field, Syd, *Screenplay: The Foundations of Screenwriting* (Delta, 2005).

Fried, Jason & and David Heinemeier Hansson, *Rework* (Crown Business, 2010).

Goldberg, Natalie, *Writing Down the Bones* (Shambhala, 2005).

Goldman, William, *Adventures in the Screen Trade* (Grand Central Publishing, 1989).

Goldman, William, *Four Screenplays* (Applause Theate and Cinema Books, 200).

Goldman, William, *Which Lie Did I Tell?* (Vintage, 2001).

Greenland, Colin, *Michael Moorcock: Death is No Obstacle* (Savoy, 1992).

King, Stephen, *On Writing* (Scriber, 2010).

Lamott, Anne, *Bird by Bird: Some Instructions on Writing and Life* (Anchor, 1995).

McCloud, Scott, *Making Comics* (William Morrow, 2006).

McKee, Robert, *Story: Substance, Structure, Style and the Principles of Screenwriting* (Regan Books, 1997).

Moorcock, Michael, *Wizardry and Wild Romance* (Monkeybrain Books, 2004).

Rand, Ken, *The 10% Solution* (Fairwood Press, 1998).

Rand, Ken, *From Idea to Story in 90 Seconds* (Fairwood Press, 2007).

Scarry, Elaine, *Dreaming by the Book* (Princeton University Press, 1999).

Smiley, Jane, *13 Ways of Looking at the Novel* (Anchor Books, 2005).

Truby, John, *The Anatomy of Story: 22 Steps to Becoming a Master Storyteller* (Faber & Faber, 2008).

Turchi, Peter, *A Muse & A Maze* (Trinity University Press, 2014).

Turchi, Peter, *Maps of the Imagination* (Trinity Univeristy Press, 2004).

Westlake, Donald E., *The Getaway Car* (University of Chicago Press, 2014).

Wilhelm, Kate, *Storyteller* (Small Beer Press, 2005).

Wood, James, *How Fiction Works* (Picador, 2008).

Tarot

Crowley, Aleister, *The Book of Thoth* (Samuel Weiser, 1944).

Greer, Mary K., *21 Ways to Read a Tarot Card* (Llewellyn Publications, 2006).

Jodorowsky, Alejandro & Marianne Costa, *The Way of Tarot* (Destiny Books, 2009).

Katz, Marcus, *Tarosophy* (Salamander and Sons, 2011).

Kenner, Corrine, *Tarot for Writers* (Llewellyn Publications, 2009).

Papus, *The Tarot of the Bohemians* (Arcanum Books, 1962).

Pollack, Rachel, *Seventy-Eight Degrees of Wisdom* (Weiser, 2007).

Pollack, Rachel, *Tarot Wisdom* (Llewellyn Publications, 2011).

Vogler, Christopher, *The Writer's Journey* (Michael Weise Productions, 1992).

Waite, Arthur Edward, *The Pictorial Key to the Tarot* (William Rider and Son, 1911).

Mythology

Campbell, Joseph, *The Hero With a Thousand Faces* (New World Library, 2008).

Eliade, Mircea, *The Myth of the Eternal Return* (Princeton University Press, 2005).

Eliade, Mircea, *The Sacred and the Profane* (Harcourt Brace Jovanovich, 2007).

Jung, Carl Gustav, *Four Archetypes* (Princeton University Press, 1970).

APPENDIX B:
DIE HARD
(a case study)

Die Hard was released in 1988, and it re-invented the action hero genre. Not only was Bruce Willis paid a record-breaking amount of money for this film (at that time; it would seem like a trivial amount compared to today's salaries), it was a risky bet on the part of Joel Silver because prior to this film, Bruce Willis was solely known as that cocky guy from *Moonlighting*.

Anyway, *Die Hard* runs approximately 132 minutes, which if we break that down into eighteen chapters, means about seven and a half minutes of screen time per chapter. If we do a quick rundown of chapter titles, it might look something like the following chart.

I've added a column for all of our boxes, and you can see how neatly the film lines up with the framework we've been working with. There are some minor variations, but for the most part, *Die Hard* nails every beat. There's a reason why it's a script that continues to be emulated to this day. Let's break this down a little more, and examine some of the beats within the chapters.

	MODEL	CHAPTER TITLE	TIME COUNT
1	PROTAGONIST	Here's John	0:00 - 7:30
2	HOOK	See John argue with Holly	7:31 - 15:00
3	ADVERSARY	Bad guys arrive	15:00 - 22:30
4		"Nice suit."	22:31 - 30:00
5	GOAL	Fire Alarm	30:01 - 37:30
6	X	"Now I have a machine gun. Ho-ho-ho"	37:31 - 45:00
7	O	Call for help	45:01 - 52:30
8	X	Where's a cop when you need one?	52:31 - 1:00:00
9	O	Bonding	1:00:01 -1:07:30
10	X	Send in SWAT	1:07:31 - 1:15:00
11	O	Someone should help SWAT out	1:15:00 - 1:22:30
12	X	"I'm your white knight."	1:22:31 - 1:31:00
13	O	Face to face	1:30:01 - 1:37:30
14	X	"I give you the FBI."	1:37:31 - 1:45:00
15	AUTHOR INTENT	"I've been a jerk."	1:45:01 - 1:52:30
16	TRANSFORMATION	Big boom	1:52:31 - 2:00:00
17	BOOM BOOM	Final Showdown	2:00:01 - 2:07:30
18	REDEMPTION	For everyone. Except Hans.	2:07:31 - 2:15:00

CHAPTER 1: Here's John

We meet John McClane on an airplane. Within the first two minutes of the film, we establish that he's a cop who has control issues, who doesn't like flying, and that he's cocky. "Trust me; I'm a cop. I've been doing this for eleven years," he says to a fellow airplane passenger who spots his gun.

John wanders down to baggage claim and meets Argyle, his limo driver. Argyle is a bit nervous because he's never driven a limo before, but John reassures Argyle that everything will be fine because he's never ridden in a limo before (the Man of the People moment). During the ride, Argyle is inquisitive and asks lots of questions, allowing the screenwriter to dump a bunch of useful back story on us about why McClane is in LA.

His wife, Holly, took a good job and moved herself and the kids to LA while John stayed behind in New York to be a cop. Without giving us any specifics, it's clear their marriage was under a lot of strain. Even in the late '80s, Holly would rather be a single woman with an executive-level career than deal with her burned-out cop husband.

John, in turn, didn't fight that Holly wanted to take the kids and move all the way across the country. He's thinks highly of her and wants to do the right thing for the everyone. But still, there's some lingering anger and resentment there, because, you know, tough guys have to shield themselves from being dumbasses.

CHAPTER 2: See John argue with Holly

During this chapter, we switch to Holly and meet her and the rest of the interesting characters at the Nakatomi Building. There's Joe Takagi, her affable boss, and Ellis, her insufferable coke-snorting associate.

John arrives at the Nakatomi Building and discovers that Holly is using her maiden name, which annoys him because it suggests that she doesn't need him any more. He goes upstairs, meets everyone, and finally gets some private time with Holly. Where she admits that she's missed him.

He says, "I see you didn't miss my name."

Because he's a jerk.

And all the old arguments come back in a flash. This happens right around the 15:00 mark.

A minute earlier, we had a brief glimpse of an anonymous van driving toward the Nakatomi Building. The music is a bit ominous, but there's nothing to see really. It's just a van. This will become important in a minute, but it isn't right now, because we're still in the midst of setting the Hook, which is: Are John and Holly going to get back together?

CHAPTER 3: Bad guys arrive

But before John and Holly can settle this argument, they're interrupted. Holly leaves to talk to the staff, and John immediately beats himself up about being an idiot.

John demonstrates his lack of emotional maturity and bounces around the executive washroom for a bit, and we leave him there while we check back in with the van that was driving up to the plaza.

The van gets cut off by a sleek sports car, which goes to the front door of the Nakatomi Building while the van disappears into the garage. It drives on down to the loading dock (passing Argyle and the parked limo, just to remind you that Argyle hasn't left the premises), and starts back up. Meanwhile, two men get out of the sports car and walk into the lobby of the building. They are animated, talking about a Lakers game, and the camera tracks along with them, giving us no time to wonder who they are or why we are watching them. And then Blam! Karl (one of the pair) shoots the man at the front desk. He darts down to the elevators and takes out the second guard. Meanwhile his pal, Theo, takes over the computer workstation and starts shutting down access to the building.

The van backs up to the loading dock, and the back opens up, disgorging a coterie of bad guys, including a well-dressed man in an overcoat. They swarm the building, continuing to lock it down.

Upstairs, McClane has taken off his shoes and is making fists with his toes on the shag carpet (just as the salesman on the airplane suggested he do as a means of stress relief). He decides that he can probably work things out with Holly, and he gets Argyle's card out of his coat and uses the phone to call down to the limo. Halfway through the call, the line goes dead.

Moments later, the bad guys arrive at the thirtieth floor and announce their presence with gunfire. Time? 23:30. The third chapter is a little long, but there's been a lot of new pieces being put in play, and we'll forgive the screen-writers for taking the time.

CHAPTER 4: "Nice suit."

We still don't know the Adversary's name, but he's clearly the well-educated and well-dressed man who takes Mr. Takagi into the boardroom to discuss the combination of the giant safe somewhere else on the floor. He quotes Shelley, mentions that he and Mr. Takagi share the same taste in suits, and then demonstrates that he isn't playing games when he shoots Mr. Takagi in the head after giving the Nakatomi executive a three-count to give up the code.

McClane, having scrambled as soon as he realized the bad guys were looking for him, has stumbled into viewing distance of the boardroom scene, and witnesses Mr. Takagi's execution. He retreats to one of the higher floors in the building, and recriminates himself for failing to save Mr. Takagi. The Adversary's goal is clearly spelled out just short of the thirty minute mark, and shortly thereafter McClane tells himself that if he had tried to save Mr. Takagi, he'd be dead too.

Now, he starts to think. He's thinking beyond just "survival," which is our default goal state for the protagonist. Now, he's thinking about stopping the bad guys and rescuing Holly (and the rest of the hostages). This is his job, after all, being the hero, and he spots the fire extinguisher heads mounted near the ceiling. There may not be walls and offices on this floor yet, but the fire safety system is definitely in place.

CHAPTERS 5 - 8: First Round of O & O

McClane triggers the fire alarm, which sends an automated signal to the local fire department, who respond with lights and sirens. We're in the second act now, and it's a long series of Obstacles and Opportunities.

• Fire Alarm triggered. (Opportunity)

• Bad Guys calls in and reports the alarm as false, and the fire engines cancel their call-out. The building monitoring system reports that the alarm came from the 35th floor. The Adversary sends men to investigate. (Obstacle)

• McClane gets in a gunfight with the man who comes to investigate. He wins, which means he now has one of the radios. And a machine gun. "Ho-ho-ho." (Opportunity)

• He sends the dead bad guy back down to the thirtieth floor, and hiding out on the elevator roof, overhears the villains talking amongst themselves. He learns stuff about them and who they are. (Opportunity)

• He heads to the roof of the building to broadcast on an emergency frequency about the situation at the Nakatomi building. The police hear him and warn him about misuse of an emergency frequency. (Obstacle)

• The Adversary hears him calling for help too, and sends Karl and another man to find him. (Obstacle)

• McClane escapes down the elevator shaft and into the ventilation system. (Opportunity)

• But Karl knows he's in the vents, and so he starts stalking McClane from room to room. (Obstacle)

• The police send a black and white patrol car to do a drive-by of the building, which makes the villains hunker down and go quiet. (Opportunity)

• The police officer who responds doesn't see anything out of the ordinary in the lobby, and leaves, intending to report that the transmission over the emergency band was a prank call. (Obstacle)

• Two more men stumble upon McClane, and he kills them both. When he sees that the black and white police car is leaving, he shoots out the window and drops one of the dead bodies on the police car. Then, just to be thorough, he shoots up the police car. (Opportunity)

CHAPTER 9: Bonding

This gets us through the next half hour of the film, each beat happening about every five minutes. We're just about halfway through the run time of the movie, and we've had a round of Obstacles and Opportunities. More pieces are put into play as the LAPD shows up and ensconces themselves around the building. An overeager TV reporter has been added to the mix, along with a self-important Deputy Chief of Police who is bound to be an ass.

Meanwhile, the Adversary insists to his men that everything is still going according to his plan, except for the fact that McClane now has the all-important detonators. And briefly, just before the one hour mark, McClane and the Adversary actually chat on the radio. First contact, which ends with McClane offering what will become his catchphrase as he disappears into the maintenance sections of the building.

And now we head into our second round of Obstacles and Opportunities, which come faster now as we're heading toward the end of Act II.

CHAPTERS 10 - 13: Second Round of O & O

• McClane has the detonators, which means the villain can't pull off his crazy plan. (Opportunity)

• Holly insists on interacting with the Adversary. "Who put you in charge?" he demands. "You did," she says. "When you shot my boss." While the connection between her and McClane is still unknown to the Adversary, he is now aware of her. (Obstacle)

• Deputy Chief of Police Dwayne T. Robinson (aka Bureaucratic Ass) sends in a SWAT team. (Opportunity)

• The bad guys are waiting, and things go poorly for our SWAT team. (Obstacle)

• SWAT doubles down by sending in an armored vehicle. (Opportunity)

• The bad guys have a rocket launcher. (Obstacle)

• McClane has C4 and a heavy CRT monitor, and an elevator shaft to drop both down. The subsequent explosion takes out the rocket launcher team. (Opportunity)

• Ellis, Mr. International Negotiator, tries to make a deal with the Adversary (who is finally named around the 1:17:00 mark). The Adversary—Hans Gruber—has a rather stark negotiating skill, and things go poorly for Ellis. (Obstacle)

• Hans finally issues his demands to the police, and the FBI show up. (Obstacle)

CHAPTER 14: "I give you the FBI"

We're now nearly three-quarters of the way through the film. There's a couple more set pieces to work through, but we need to start tightening things up. In fact, in the very next scene, McClane learns what the detonators are for (blowing up the roof), and he meets Hans. McClane is fooled by Hans's sniveling executive bit and he thinks Hans is one of the Nakatomi executives who got missed in all the excitement. So, for a moment, they're pals and we have a bit of bonding.

Of course, Hans is just waiting for his chance, and shortly thereafter, everyone is shooting at each other again, and it is back to business as usual. Except, McClane loses the detonators and gets a piece of glass shoved into his foot. Drat.

Meanwhile, Theo hits the last lock on the vault, which he can't crack. He needs a Christmas miracle. Hans replies, "You ask for a miracle; I give you the FBI." Who are busy following the terrorist handbook: cut the power; bring in attack choppers.

CHAPTER 15: "I've been a jerk."

McClane does his best to bandage up his wounded foot, and has one last conversation with Al Powell, wherein he asks Powell to find his wife when this all over and tell her that he (McClane) has been a jerk. This is his transformative reveal (right at 1:46:00), and all he wants is to say that he's sorry for all the pain he's caused both of them over the last few years. Heartfelt, honest, and right where we're expecting to find this revelation.

Shortly thereafter, McClane is ambushed by a couple of the bad guys, including Karl, who wants revenge for the first man that McClane killed (Karl's brother—all very neat and tidy). The obnoxious TV reporter gets on the air and reveals that McClane has family in LA, and Hans makes the connection between Holly and McClane, taking her as his personal hostage.

CHAPTER 16: Big Boom

The attack helicopters show up.

McClane gets the hostages off the roof; Hans hits the detonators, and blows the roof, destroying one of the helicopters.

It's all chaos and fire and emergency lighting as the surviving bad guys finish raiding the vault of the millions of bearer bonds.

CHAPTER 17: Final Showdown

But then McClane shows up, looking like crap (as the action hero always does by the end), and there's one final stand-off, wherein the tables are turned on Hans and his henchman by some well-applied duct tape, and everyone gets what they always wanted.

Except Hans.

It's a good thing he got all the best dialogue.

APPENDIX C:
NARRATIVE ARC BY TAROT

I LIKE TO USE A TAROT DECK THAT HAS IMAGES THAT ARE representative of the genre of the book that I'm planning to write because the art of the cards helps put my creative brain in the right headspace book. Occasionally, after I do one reading, I'll get one or two more decks out and replicate the reading with those decks. Just to put a wide variety of visual magic in front of my eyeballs. Your mileage may vary.

A deck rich with symbols and colors is always preferred, and unless you have a specific relationship with one of the more common decks (the Rider-Waite or some version of the Marseille deck), I do recommend picking up a deck that is a little out of your comfort zone (both in images and in understanding of all the symbols). This will force you to dig a little deeper in order to parse the cards.

After taking a moment to clear my head, I deal ten cards in the Celtic Cross layout, and I got the following spread:

1. THE HEART - ACE OF WANDS
2. THE ADVERSARY - QUEEN OF SWORDS

3. THE ROOT - LUST
4. THE PAST - EMPRESS
5. THE VISION - NINE OF SWORDS
6. THE FUTURE - ACE OF SWORDS
7. THE MIRROR - FOUR OF PENTACLES
8. THE EYE - KNIGHT OF WANDS
9. THE GUIDE - TWO OF WANDS
10. THE OUTCOME - THE MOON

What sort of patterns can we see? There are lots of wands and swords. Wands are the suit of fire, and swords are the suit of air, and air comes about because of a conjunction of fire and water, which sets up a hierarchy of the swords being subservient to the wands—and there's a source of conflict right there. The Queen of Swords is laid across the Ace of Wands, suggesting, again, the adversarial struggle between swords and wands.

There are three Major Arcana cards: Lust (or Strength), the Empress, and the Moon. In the Thoth deck designed by Aleister Crowley (which I used for the first pass at this reading), Strength is renamed to Lust because Crowley believed the card to signify more than just strength; for him, it also signified the joy of strength being exercised. There's a hedonist element to Crowley's Lust (naturally), which suggests dominance in a sexual manner or strength used to control versus strength used to uplift.

The Thoth deck has a wealth of symbolism woven into all of the cards, but many of the interpretations can quickly stray from virtue to vice through over-indulgence. We have Lust for the Root and the Empress for the Past, suggesting that our protagonist has come from a realm that is indulgent in its embrace. A person of money and means, perhaps.

Our outcome is the Moon, which is the threat of over-indulgence realized. The Moon is the threshold of madness, but it is also the gate to radical creativity. This is the gate through which the artist must pass during their transformative arc. The Moon symbolizes the entirety of the passage through the Underworld in the Campbellian interpretation. Whoever our protagonist is, they're going to be launched into darkness.

The Empress is also a gate, so we have passage from one realm into the realm of the immediate story, and then on to the realm beyond the threshold of madness.

Above and in front of the protagonist we have two sword cards—the ace and the nine—matching in opposition the two Major Arcana cards. Both are suggestive of the primordial state of air. In the case of the nine, it is the power of air returning to rest. Disorder is now rectified. Chaos has been calmed. This is the vision—what the protagonist wants. In the immediate future, though, is the purest form of air. It's the state before disorder and chaos, and so the question this card raises is what actions on the part of the protagonist cause a change in the calm order of air so that they seek a return to that state?

Frankly, this is the basic structure of the Hero's Journey: our hero finds their world out of balance, so they leave that heretofore Edenic state and travel through the under-world, seeking the boon that will rescue their world. Once the boon is received, they return, and all is well again. So, it seems like we're setting up a narrative of a journey that is sticking fairly close to the Hero's Journey.

So what have we got along the way? The four of penta-cles is the Mirror—the protagonist as they are seen by the world at large. The four of pentacles is usually represented as a quartet of pyramids that protect a precious center. They are law and order, under constant vigilance. Then we have the knight of wands, who is the fiery part of fire, which is both good and bad. He's the guy who will never give up on his mission, but he's not the brightest thinker in the bunch, which means that if his original effort is flawed in some manner, he's got nothing in his saddlebags that is going to save him. He's the guy who will charge off the cliff because it is there and he doesn't know how to turn his horse.

And then we have the two of wands, which is the state of fire after the ace. If the ace is the primordial idea of fire—fire before fire—then the two is that fire given intent. It is the fire that burns and destroys, because before you create you have to separate. You have to destroy something before you have any pieces to work with.

It's a reading that suggests our protagonist is doomed in his quest, or that he's questing for something that is going to turn out to not quite be the boon he thinks it is. The Queen of Swords is gracious and benevolent, but she's also capricious and sly. She's not averse to seducing you to her side, and then sending you off to do her dirty work without telling you that said work involves killing puppies.

Even with all of this, I didn't have a solid idea of who the protagonist was, and so I drew one more card to give me a clearer representation of this individual. I drew the Sun—the Major Arcana card that represents the pure Blakean child—one who has made the journey from innocence to experience and back again. The child who has escaped Philip K. Dick's black iron prison and is ready to emerge into the world again. In Egyptian mythology, this child is Horus, who is born from the union of Osiris, the death and resurrection god, and Isis—the mother goddess figure. Osiris was slain by Set, in one of the age-old wars between the Hero and the Adversary, and Set dismembered Osiris, scattering the pieces of the slain god across the world. Isis gathered them all up,[47] and brought Osiris back to life enough for a child to be conceived. Horus is the man Osiris can no longer be,[48] and it is Horus who sends Set packing.

So, the sun. Or, the son. Depending on how you want to look at it.

Which makes me think of *Hamlet.* And *Oedipus.*

---

47. Except for his penis, because what's a good bit of world-building without a castration motif to keep the young lads in line?

48. Which basically translates to "Kids, if you're dead AND missing your junk, you're probably never going to be king again. Give up the crown to someone who has a little more going for them."

On the deck I'm using, the Queen of Swords is holding a severed head in one hand, and she's got a sword in the other. I think she's slain her husband in order to take the throne for herself. But in whatever world this is, she can't rule without a king, so she seeks a consort who will be malleable and subservient. Enter our protagonist, untested and unproven on the field of battle and in the chambers of love and politics. Is he the queen's son? That's a little twitchy, but what if he is a clone of the dead king? A piece of the old man, grown in a vat under the strict order of the queen. He is poured out into the world (the gate of the empress, if you will), where he must be blooded and tested in order to fully come into his heritage. He is, at the beginning, an idea without form. He comes into the world—did the queen set this plan in motion during sexual congress with her husband?—and wants nothing more than to be the best son/king ever. At this point, he is the ace of swords: perfectly poised to do . . . something.

And so he does. He leaves the safety of his perfect world (the four of pentacles), intent on his mission for his queen (the knight of wands), but somewhere along the way, he becomes clued in to the machinations going on around him. He's like Hamlet who discovers that his mother, the queen, has slain his father, but she doesn't want to put some other dude on the throne, she wants to put him on the throne, because he is a purified version of his father. Yeah for the magic of genetic engineering!

Naturally, this makes our protagonist a bit bonkers.

This narrative arc is missing the third act, but I can go to Hamlet for that final structure if I still need it when I've gotten to that point in the book. And yes, this does feel like *Hamlet* meets *Oedipus* IN SPACE, but Shakespeare gives us the go-ahead in regards to recycling material in his fifty-ninth sonnet.

> *If there be nothing new, but that which is*
> *Hath been before, how are our brains beguil'd,*
> *Which, labouring for invention, bear amiss*
> *The second burden of a former child.*

What is old is new again in about fifteen years (witness the endless spate of remakes and reboots in television and film), so don't worry too much about leaning on source material. Stories are enriched because they extend back through our cultural and literary heritages. But whatever you do use for foundation stones, make sure you mix the mortar a little differently, because you are different than all the writers who have gone before. You're different than me and that weirdo on the bus and all those marvelous readers out there who are waiting for another book from you.

Be inventive. We use the known structures and the mythological models because they are familiar and our audiences like the comfort of familiarity, but stamp them with your passion and your quirky sense of humor and your passion. Stamp them so very hard with your passion.

ACKNOWLEDGMENTS

THE FOLLOWING PEOPLE WERE PART OF A DOMINO EFFECT which ultimately ends with the publication of this book.

Les Howle asked me to do a panel at Norwescon one night while we were sitting in an airport lounge, waiting for our flight. I came up with an idea and pitched it. She said yes. Norwescon gave me a big room and two hours, and I filled it. Thanks also to Karen Junker, who came up to me immediately after this panel and asked me to reprise it for the Cascade Writers conference the following summer, and H. R. Ruolo, who blogged about the Norwescon panel and would tell me several years later that it was continually one of her highest traffic blog posts. Les Howle also got me the gig with Clarion West, where I turned the two hour version of this talk into a full day workshop.

Sandra Wickham invited me to be the Guest of Honor at the first Creative Ink Festival, which was an opportunity for me to try out the new structure for this content. The talk was a success, and this book was a natural progression. Thank you, Sandra, for trusting me to be entertaining enough to launch your Festival.

Evelyn Nicholas reminded me on a regular basis that I should be writing more, and for that she should be eternally commended.

Patrick Swenson suffered through many lengthy conversations where I thought through portions of this model. Well, let's be honest here. They were more like rambling monologues than actual conversations, but he nodded and make grunting noises at appropriate times, which was greatly appreciated.

Darin Bradley, Misti Morrison, Aaron Leis, and Rima Abunasser (aka the Texas Office) were co-participants in more than one wild hunt for the creative muse, and I appreciate their willingness to explore uncharted territory.

Neal Von Flue, who has consistently demonstrated a great deal of enthusiasm for creating art to go along with my words, provided the iconic illustrations to go along with the Nine Box Outline Model. He is a saint, and mulit-talented beyond his mere skills with a pencil.

Erica Sage brooked no bullshit and no whining, which is only payback for when I have taken that tone with her. This is how writers show affection for one another.

ABOUT THE AUTHOR

I'VE WRITTEN THRILLERS, URBAN FANTASY, EROTIC ROMANCE, historical adventure stories, ghost stories, experimental WTF? projects, comic scripts, movie scripts, and a lot of marketing copy. I've run a transmedia property (*The Fore-world Saga*), which had books, novellas, comics, movie scripts, TV scripts, and game narratives.

I've edited, rewritten, ghost-written, pitched, made up wild cover copy, nodded sagely at words written by better writers than I, and run group brainstorm sessions that have done and undone an entire season's worth of work in two or three sessions. I wrote five distinct versions of my second novel because I didn't know how to line edit.

I write fewer drafts now.

My full CV is at my website, under the ABOUT section, in case you are curious about the work I've done.[49]

My twitter handle is @markteppo.

In this regard, I try to be easy to find.

In addition to all this writing and creating, I own a media umbrella company called Firebird Creative. There

---

49. Or use this URL: http://markteppo.com/projects/teppo_CV.pdf

are a number of publishing imprints associated with the company. You can find out about the various books and projects at the website (http://firebirdcreative.net).

I'm always delighted to hear feedback about the process outlined in this book, so please feel free to drop me a note at darkline@gmail.com and let me know. While working on this book, I've come to realize there may be other ways to apply the Nine Box Outline Model to creative processes, and so I'm especially interested in feedback regarding a continuation of this series into other aspects of writing.

I do have a mailing list. You'll get one or two emails a month, which will mostly be teasers of new content, updates on what I'm working on, and useful writing tips.

You can sign up at http://markteppo.com/mailing-list.

LEAVING FEEDBACK

IF YOU'VE FOUND THIS BOOK TO BE USEFUL, PLEASE LEAVE A review at your favorite online venue (Goodreads, Shelfari, Amazon, Barnes & Noble, et cetera). Reviews and stars mean a lot to independent writers as they are the metric by which they are judged by the all-mighty and all-knowing algorithm. While buying a second copy of this book and giving it to a friend is a delightful and welcome reaction to the words herein, leaving a review and a rating is also greatly appreciated.

Stars = Love.

Shameless, I know. But it's what makes the world go 'round these days.

We can be rebels when it comes to our punctuation, but let's play the game when it comes to showing the love for authors.

And I'm not asking just for myself. Go give some stars to someone else whose book you've loved. Do it. I know it'll feel good.

Made in the USA
Columbia, SC
14 October 2022

69284054R00086